THE DUTIES

OF THE

CHRISTIAN MINISTRY;

WITH A VIEW OF THE

PRIMITIVE AND APOSTOLICAL CHURCH,

AND THE DANGER OF DEPARTURE FROM ITS DOCTRINE AND DISCIPLINE.

A SERMON,

PREACHED AT AN ORDINATION HELD IN THE CHURCH OF
ST. PETER, COLOMBO,

BY GEORGE TREVOR, LORD BISHOP OF MADRAS.

BY

THE REV. B. BAILEY, M.A.,

SENIOR COLONIAL CHAPLAIN OF THE ISLAND OF CEYLON.

WITH

Notes and an Appendix,

CONTAINING COPIOUS EXTRACTS FROM VARIOUS AUTHORS.

LONDON:

WILLIAM EDWARD PAINTER, 342, STRAND.

"Nemini enim dubium esse potest, quin universalis Ecclesiæ fidei moribusque in omnibus, quoad fieri potest, religiosé insistere, et tutissimum sit, et summé necessarium.

For no one can doubt, but that it is most safe, and supremely necessary, in all things, as far as is possible, religiously to walk in the steps of the faith and customs of the Universal Church."—Preface to *Codex Canonum Ecclesiæ Primitivæ vindicatus ac illustratus, Autore Gulielmo Beveregio, Ecclesiæ Anglicanæ Presbytero.* London, 1678. Reprinted in vol. ii. of Cotelerius's edition of the "Apostolic Fathers."

TO

THE RIGHT REVEREND GEORGE TREVOR,

LORD BISHOP OF MADRAS,

𝕿𝖍𝖎𝖘 𝖘𝖊𝖗𝖒𝖔𝖓,

PREACHED AND PUBLISHED AT HIS REQUEST,

IS,

WITH MUCH ESTEEM AND REGARD,

RESPECTFULLY INSCRIBED,

BY

HIS FAITHFUL AND AFFECTIONATE SERVANT,

THE AUTHOR.

CONTENTS.

	PAGE
Address	v
Sermon	19
Appendix	71
Preface to Appendix	73
Note A. Apostolical Succession	83
B. Who is the Heretic?	106
C. Principles of the Church of England	107
D. Of the Word "Priest"	116
E. The Three Orders of Christian Ministry	122
F. The Church of Christ	126
G. Calvin and the Genevan Reformers	131
H. Creeds of the Church; and the Episcopal Churches of Sweden and Norway, and of Denmark and Iceland	141
I. The overthrow of Episcopacy in Scotland	186
K. Bishop Horne's Opinion of the Scotch Episcopal Church	197
L. Universality of the Catholic Church	200
M. The Free Constitution of the Church	203
N. Bishops Middleton and Heber	207
O. The True Spirit of the Church of England	219
P. Religious Opinions of Saxony, Prussia, and Germany, during the 18th Century	223
Q. Present State of Religion in Germany and Prussia	225
R. Infidelity of Scotch Metaphysicians—Hume, Bolingbroke, and Gibbon; and the Metaphysical Tendency of Calvin's Peculiar Doctrines	247

CONTENTS.

	PAGE
Note S. Innovations of Calvin	273
T. The Socinianism of the Church of Geneva	287
U. Tendency of Calvinistic Predestination and Low Church Principles to Socinianism; and the contrary Tendency of Mahometan Heresies to Trinitarianism	292
V. The Importance of Personal Religion to the Ministers of Christ	302
W. Directions as to the conduct of the Native Ministers in the conversion of, and ministration among, the Native Inhabitants of Ceylon: (communicated by a Native Clergyman)	306
X. Theological Studies	318
SUPPLEMENT	327
I. Apostolical Succession	329
On Separation, and the State of Foreign Churches	331
Foreign Churches not Heretical and Schismatical	335
II. Union of the Word of God and the Church of God	341
III. The Reformation, Presbyterianism, and Episcopacy	346
IV. Ancient Literature, and the first Native Bishop of Iceland	384

TO THE LORD BISHOP OF MADRAS.

My Lord,

The approbation with which your Lordship honoured this Sermon has stamped upon it a value to which, of itself, it has no title. Your impression may, moreover, give it a circulation which otherwise it would not have. I have laid down certain principles, for which some readers may require proof. I have asserted some important facts, which by others may be thought to demand illustration.

A concise statement and a condensed argument are enough for clergymen. The subjects of their studies and their habits of thought render it easy to them to fill up the outline. The public have a right to demand something more demonstrative. I have, therefore, in the Appendix, endeavoured to throw together such facts and other illustrations as bear upon the subject-matter of the discourse.

Permit me, my Lord, to avail myself of the present opportunity to advert to the circumstance which gave rise to the following pages. I refer to your Lordship's recent and primary Visitation of your clergy in this island. You found us almost as sheep without a shepherd. With the solitary exception of your lamented predecessor in the see of Madras, who did not live to make himself personally acquainted with his Ceylon clergy, our chief pastors and diocesans have hitherto been the Bishops of Calcutta. Their distance precluded the possibility of frequent or prolonged visitations to this remote part of that immense diocese. Your Lordship is the first Bishop of Madras who has visited Ceylon. Five years had elapsed since the last Episcopal visitation, by the present Bishop of Calcutta, our respected Metropolitan.

The excellency, the beauty, and the safeguard of Episcopacy consist in a combination of the energies of the clergy under the paternal sway of the bishop. The Church, I am persuaded, can never prosper without the frequent presence, as well as the constant and vigilant superintendence, of the bishops in their several dioceses. Thus, under their continual and paternal sway, as under the primitive fathers of the Catholic Church, no true Churchman—no enlightened Christian, can doubt that, with God's blessing, our work will be crowned with final success.

"The faith of a true Churchman (remarks one who has won for himself that honourable title) will lead him to believe that the blessing of God will ultimately rest on the labours of all who seek to advance *God's* cause in the manner appointed by *God* himself. The instruments may be dishonoured, the agents may be subjected either to the physical persecution of Queen Mary's reign [in England], or to that moral persecution which, in the present age, is directed against all true Churchmen—but the cause will prosper."*

In this remote and insular part of your Lordship's diocese we are not exempted from the ordeal of "moral persecution," which in England is the trial of consistent Churchmen. But we, too, believe and trust "that the blessing of God will ultimately rest on our labours," and that "the cause will prosper."

It has been my humble endeavour, in the following discourse, to demonstrate that the Episcopacy of our venerable Establishment is identical with the divinely-instituted order of Church government which prevailed *universally* in the earliest and

---

* Preface to "The Early Life and Professional Years of Bishop Hobart." By Walter Farquhar Hook, D.D., &c. &c.

purest ages of Christianity, and which was undisturbed for fifteen hundred years subsequent to the birth of Christ, and was received by all men, and in all places, of the Christian world, as the Catholic and Apostolical Church.

Of Episcopacy, therefore, as of other Catholic verities, the rule of Vincentius holds good.—*In ipsâ item Catholicâ Ecclesiâ magnoperé curandum est, ut id teneamus, quod ubique, quod semper, quod ab omnibus, creditum est.* I have further endeavoured to show, and have supported my assertions by historical facts in the Appendix, the dangerous errors and heresies into which Christian countries have fallen, and in which some of them now are, by the act of having thrown off this divine and primitive order of the government of the Church of Christ.

In the primitive and in many subsequent ages of Christianity it entered the mind of no one to dispute, for an instant, this divine foundation of the visible Church upon the Apostles and Prophets, Jesus Christ himself being the chief corner stone. But in the age in which we live it would seem to require some courage to withstand the "moral persecution" of being branded with bigotry, intolerance, and uncharitableness, when we boldly and uncompromisingly assert this fundamental principle. But, blessed be God! in spite of the almost fierce intolerance, for so it is, of the ultra-Protestant spirit of the age, the ranks of true Churchmen are fast filling up. It is indeed a crisis of deep interest; but the fearless and firm, yet calm upholders of primitive truth and primitive usages, are daily coming forth.

At this day, my Lord, consistent Churchmen, who intrepidly assert the principles of that church or society, whose doctrine and discipline, of which our Episcopal government may be fitly deemed a portion or an appurtenance, they are bound by the strongest ties of heaven and earth to maintain—consistent Churchmen, I say, are charged with bigotry, intolerance, and a host of secular and unworthy passions and feelings. Be it so. Conscious rectitude of purpose can bear much more. We have counted the cost—we have searched our hearts. With the blessing and the grace of God, we will not abandon our post. Let them who would thus stigmatize Churchmen reflect whether they be not stirred by a yet deeper spirit of intolerance than that which they charge upon us? But let us humbly examine our own hearts, whether these things be so; and let us guard against the intrusion of such unhallowed feelings within the sanctuary. *Humile sapiamus.*

The claim of apostolical succession by the Episcopalian is affirmed to be the uncharitable presumption of intolerance, because it infers that other communities are not properly churches, but sects, and that their ministers are not duly and regularly authorized. The inference is unavoidable. But the facts on which this claim is grounded must be overthrown, before the alleged intolerance can, with any shadow of justice, be maintained. Are they true, or are they false? This is the state of the question.

"The opponent of Episcopacy may dispute the fact, but the Episcopalian must hold it, or he ceases to be an Episcopalian. Nor can he be accused of want of charity for so doing, any more than (the objector) himself, if he asserts, which probably he may, that some doctrines are essential to salvation. The Trinitarian is equally uncharitable on this principle, since he condemns the Socinian; the Socinian because he condemns the Deist; the Deist because he condemns the Atheist. The true Christian feels that it is his duty to maintain the *whole* truth as it is in Jesus, to declare the whole counsel of God. If, in so doing, consequences may seem to result from his doctrine, which he may shrink from maintaining, his answer is—'Such is the truth, and I assert it; such the rule, to which exceptions *may* be made, though I am not authorized to declare them; such the counsel of God; as to the rest, I condemn no man, though I may believe him to be dangerously in error, because I am commanded not to judge.'"*

I have, my Lord, a few words more, and but a few to offer in reference to your recent, and too brief, visit to our island. You have won the hearts of the people of all ranks, among whom you came, by your kindness and urbanity, your conciliating manners

---

* Dr. Hook, ut supra.

and your truly Christian deportment. You have afflicted them only by their painful sympathy for the severe bodily suffering, with which, during your sojourn among them, it pleased God to visit you. They perceived, nevertheless, that, in spite of this obvious state of suffering and debility, you persisted, to the overtasking of your strength, in the resolute discharge of your sacred functions. They do you ample justice for the ardour of your zeal, your sincere devotion to your high and holy calling. We know, my Lord, by whom, and on what occasion it was said—

"Καλὸν δὲ τὸ ζηλοῦσθαι ἐν καλῷ παντοτε."*

May we, your Lordship's clergy, imitate your example; and may we

* Gal. iv. 18.

lay to heart the delicate reproof of the holy apostle to the Galatians in the passage of which the above-cited words are a portion. May we never relax our exertions in our holy calling, whether our bishop be absent or present with us—whether the circumstances and situation in which we live and labour be prosperous or adverse, propitious or discouraging.

And that it may please the Almighty Father of all to restore your Lordship to your wonted health and strength, or to such a measure of them as may enable you without pain to discharge your important functions; and that with frequency, and for a longer period, you may visit this portion of your diocese, is, I am strongly persuaded, the earnest desire and the prayer of the Christian community, the laity as well as the clergy, of the island of Ceylon; and I need scarcely add, of none more sincerely and devotedly than, my Lord,

Your Lordship's
Faithful and affectionate
servant,
B. BAILEY.

COLUMBO, March 9, 1840.

SERMON, &c.

"Study to show thyself approved unto God, a workman that needeth not to be ashamed, rightly dividing the word of truth."—2 *Timothy* ii. 15.

To address an audience such as that which is now assembled within these sacred walls, of which the bishop and my brethren the clergy are a conspicuous part; to be called upon by my superior to do this, as an act of duty, in the way of exhortation to those, some of whom could more fittingly and ably, both by precept and example, afford admonition and instruction to myself; to endeavour to throw a faint light upon the feet of persons* about to be invested with the sacred office of messengers of the

* Native candidates for orders about to be ordained as Church missionaries.

blessed tidings of salvation to the heathen people of this island, who sit in darkness and the shadow of death; to offer encouragement and consolation to all who, by the laying on of apostolic hands, will be this day enrolled among the authorized ministers of Christ; this is a duty involving so deep and solemn responsibility, that it were to betray an utter insensibility and a culpable self-reliance not to feel and to acknowledge a painful diffidence of my ability to perform, in any adequate degree, my difficult and allotted task.

It *is*, however, a duty; and it must be performed, relying on higher power, to the best of my ability. Imploring, therefore, the divine blessing on my weak endeavours, I shall proceed to lay down and enforce the arduous and responsible duties of a FAITHFUL MINISTER OF CHRIST.

But I shall begin, by way of introduction, with a brief view of the primitive Catholic and Apostolical Church, whereby, it is hoped, a true value may be affixed to the sacred and solemn offices with which our brethren, who are here present as candidates for orders, will be invested ere they leave this hallowed building. I shall conduct this enquiry by the light of the inspired Scripture. The primary steps in the formation of a visible Church, afterwards carried out by the immediate successors of the apostles, are to be distinctly traced in the pages of the New Testament by every eye which is at all instructed in that sacred volume, except it be wilfully closed against it, or involuntarily denied by prejudice and sectarian associations. It is especially so in the two Epistles to Timothy, in that to Titus, and in other parts and passages of this great apostle's invaluable writings. These truths are surely portions of " the things" thus emphatically mentioned by St. Paul at the commencement of the second chapter of his second Epistle to Timothy, whence our text is selected : " Thou therefore, my son, be strong in the grace that is in Christ

Jesus. And THE THINGS that thou hast heard of me among many witnesses, the same commit thou to FAITHFUL MEN, who shall be able to teach others also."*

But while it is my more immediate duty to press the awful responsibility of that ministerial office, and "the things" now about to be "committed" to our brethren, who, I pray God, will be found "faithful men;" while I would impress *them* with deep and solemn feelings on this most affecting and momentous era of their earthly pilgrimage, I would, if I might be allowed, avail myself of the present occasion the more earnestly and affectionately, in the presence of our respected and esteemed bishop, to bring before the minds and consciences of *ourselves*, my reverend brethren, who have been—some of us long time—presbyters of the Church of Christ, the dying injunction of this holy apostle to "his dearly beloved son Timothy."† I

---

* 2 Tim. ii. 1, 2.   See Appendix, Note A.
† See his salutation in the second Epistle to Timo-

would ask ourselves whether we can hope to be accounted "faithful men," worthy of this sacred deposit—this mighty trust? I would, if I were enabled by God's blessing, awaken in our own bosoms, my brethren, a solemn, a profound, a reverential sense of our own ordination vows, and of the awful obligations we then bound upon our spirits; of all which we must give a solemn account at the great day. And which one of us, I would further ask, when in a proper frame of mind and spirit—which God grant!—can read, or hear, without deep emotion, nay, without awe, the thrilling charge of the dying apostle to Timothy, in the concluding chapter of his second Epistle, and the very last of those divinely inspired compositions which he bequeathed to the Church:—"I charge

thy, so much more warm and personally affectionate than that of the first Epistle. In the first, Timothy is styled, "my own son in the faith;" in the second, "my dearly beloved son," as suitable to the occasion of their final separation in this world, and until they should be re-united in the world of the sainted spirits of those who had departed in the Lord.

thee, before God and the Lord Jesus Christ, who shall judge the quick and the dead at His appearing and His kingdom, preach the word; be instant in season, out of season; reprove, rebuke, exhort, with all long-suffering and doctrine?"*

In conformity with these various and solemn injunctions of the great Apostle to the Gentiles, the eminently wise and excellent compilers of our inimitable Liturgy, which is the traditionary piety of the earliest and purest ages of the Christian Church,† collated and defecated of all the impurities of the superstitious and he-

---

* 2 Tim. iv. 1, 2.

† Along with Comber, Wheatly, and other well known works on the Book of Common Prayer, the reader may consult with advantage the following works, among others, upon ancient Liturgies:— Comber's "History of the Primitive and General Use of Liturgies;" Brett's "Collection of the Principal Liturgies," &c.; Bingham's "Origines Ecclesiasticæ," volumes v. vi.; Bishop Sparrow's "Rationale of the Common Prayer," of which, as well as of Bingham's works, I am rejoiced to observe reprints in England; and Mr. Palmer's work, "The Antiquities of the English Ritual," &c., two volumes 8vo. Oxford, 1832. No clergyman ought to be without this last work on his shelves.

retical* mixtures of the Romish Church—the compilers of our Liturgy have enjoined, in the rubrics of the ordination services, that, before the bishop proceeds to the ordination of the persons to be presented, there be delivered "a sermon or exhortation, declaring the duty and office of such as come to be admitted deacons and priests; how necessary these orders are in the Church of Christ, and also how the people ought to esteem them in their offices."

This is that duty which I am now called upon, however unworthy, to perform. I shall then, in the first place, so far follow the rubric as to give a very brief view, rather a slender outline, of the constitution of the Church of Christ, of which the Church of England is a not inconsiderable branch, and of the origin and necessity of those two orders of deacon and priest, in conjunction with the first, the episcopal order: and it is to be hoped and prayed

* See Appendix, Note B.

that the people of the Church, and the congregation, who form the great *body* of the Church, cannot fail to esteem highly in the Lord these ministers in their several offices, while they conscientiously perform their sacred functions.

The Church, of which ministers of the two inferior orders are about to be ordained by the laying on of hands and the authority of the bishop, is a spiritual society, composed of Christian nations. It is called *Catholic*, in contradistinction to the Jewish Church; because it is the universal Church of every nation upon earth. "My house shall be called, of all nations, the house of prayer,"[*] is the language of the Saviour himself. All nations, and the people of each nation, ought to be of one Church: and were we in such a state of spiritual advancement as to be agreed upon doctrine and discipline, all who name the name of Christ would communicate with each

---

[*] Mark xi. 17. Compare 1 Kings viii. 29; Isaiah lvi. 7.

other in one Catholic or Universal Church. God has permitted it to be otherwise. But being of one Catholic and Apostolic, or Episcopal Church, we must not, on this account, lose sight of first principles, while we must be freely and charitably tolerant of all other denominations. The best and only safe mode of being charitable to others is to be true to ourselves. None of us, on fitting occasions like the present, should, if he have any love for the Church or respect for himself, shrink from the open and bold avowal of his own principles.*

As every society must have rulers or governors, and ministers or officers, so the spiritual society, the Church, has its rulers and its ministers. These are threefold. Bishops, the first order, are its rulers. Under them, presbyters, or priests,† are overseers of the flock, administering the sacraments, praying for the people, and

---

* See Appendix, Note C.
† See Appendix, Note D.

preaching the word of God: these comprehend the second order. Deacons are the third order.

It is, moreover, the received doctrine, upon this subject, of all of our communion, and of other Episcopal Churches, such as the Greek and the Romish, not in communion with us, that, since the modelling of a visible Church, or spiritual society, according to the Levitical law, under Aaron, the first high priest of the Hebrews, with the two orders of priests and Levites under him, no Church, or society, can be strictly intitled to that denomination, which has not this threefold order of ministry, of which the Hebrew Church is the model.* The law indeed, in all senses, external and internal, is the schoolmaster to bring us unto Christ. Christian Churches, moreover, that they may have a just claim to the title, must have a regular succession of ministers from the times of the Apostles,

* See Appendix, Note E.

and the first planting of the Churches by apostolical hands.*

To the Apostles it was commanded by our Lord himself: "Go ye, therefore, and teach all nations, baptizing them in the name of the Father, and of the Son, and of the Holy Ghost; teaching them to observe all things whatsoever I have commanded you: and, lo, I am with you alway, even to the end of the world."† It was to the Apostles, moreover, that Christ gave the keys of the kingdom of heaven, saying, "Whatsoever ye shall bind on earth shall be bound in heaven; and whatsoever ye shall loose on earth shall be loosed in heaven."‡ And as it has been further remarked by a learned writer, and one deeply skilled in Christian antiquities, "They were the Apostles alone whom Christ sent, as His Father sent Him, with authority to govern that kingdom which

---

* See Ante Appendix, Note A.

† Matt. xxviii. 19, 20.   ‡ Matt. xvi. 19.

He had purchased with His blood. As He knew all things, He was fully aware that the Apostles were mortal, and that, in fact, none of them would long survive the approaching destruction of Jerusalem. It could not, therefore, be with themselves personally, but with their successors in office from age to age, that He was to be alway, even to the end of the world."*

Many of the ordinances, and the sacrificial and other rites, such as the paschal lamb, and the feast of the passover, and others in the Mosaic law, typify and adumbrate the life, death, religion, and other circumstances of Christ. It was so in the form and fabric of the Church itself. The Jewish Church was, as it were, the platform on which the visible Church of Christ, as well as the spiritual, was constructed. It likewise was built on " Apostles and

---

* Appendix I. to Mosheim's Ecclesiastical History, vol. vi., p. 90. London, 1811.—See Appendix, Note F.

Prophets, Jesus Christ himself being the chief corner stone."

While Christ was upon earth, and after that He had entered upon His ministry, He himself was high priest, and the antitype of the Jewish high priest. He called and sent forth twelve Apostles, according to the number of the heads of the twelve tribes, to preach the Gospel. He invested them with governing or judicial power. He declared that they should sit on twelve thrones, judging the twelve tribes of Israel. He next sent forth seventy disciples, which were as the seventy elders—a court constituted to assist Moses in the administration of the affairs of Israel. But no power of government, as to the twelve Apostles, was assigned to the seventy elders. They were appointed simply to preach the Gospel, confirmed by the signs following of working miracles.

The first act of the Apostles, as governors of the Church, after the ascension of their Divine Master, was the appointment of deacons.* This third order, the Apostles being the first, completed the ministry. It thus continued universally in the Church, without interruption, for fifteen hundred years. And although the reformation of the Western Church, early in the sixteenth century, broke this continuity among many of the Protestant communities, and divided them into separate sects, in Germany,† Holland, Switzerland,‡ and parts of France,‡ among the sectaries in England, and ultimately in Scotland, as a national establishment; the primitive and apostolical government of the Catholic Church of Christ has never been abandoned by the Church of England, by far the most influential and important Church

---

* Acts vi. 1-3.

† For the progress and establishment of the Reformation in the united provinces of Holland in the sixteenth century, and for the various sects of the Dutch in the seventeenth century, see Mosheim's Ecclesiastical History, vol. iv., p. 126, and vol. v., p. 434; and for the state of the Dutch Church in 1816, see "A Tour through Belgium and Holland," by James Mitchel, M.A., p. 217. London, 1816.

‡ See Appendix, Note G.

in the present world. The proper denomination of the Church of England, and of all Reformed Churches retaining their Episcopacy, is THE REFORMED CATHOLIC CHURCH.* The Church of Sweden,† though Lutheran in doctrine, is the only other national Church of the Reformers

---

* "The absurdity is at once apparent of the Romish Dissenters from the Church of England, when they accuse us of doing what they have done themselves— of having departed or dissented from the old Church, and of having reared a new Church of merely human origin. The absurdity is great of the English Papists, when they speak of their sect as the old Church and the old religion. The present Church of England is the old Catholic Church of England, reformed in the reigns of Henry, Edward, and Elizabeth, and cleansed of certain superstitious errors; it is the same Church which came down from our British and Saxon ancestors; and as such it possesses its original endowments, which were never, as some persons foolishly suppose, taken from our Church and given to another. And it was not till the tenth year of Elizabeth that, at the instigation of foreign emissaries, a small party separated itself, and, dissenting from the Catholic Church of England, formed the Romish sect in this country. We did not go out from them, but they went out from us. The Church of England, then—that Church which is still established in this country—is the old Catholic Church which was originally planted in this country."—*Preface to the Early Life and Professional Years of Bishop Hobart*, pp. 15, 16.

† See Appendix, Note H.

which perhaps purely adhered to the apostolical government, by an uninterrupted succession, of the three orders of ministry. Scotland wavered; and finally, through political faction, she broke off, as a national establishment. But until the last rebellion of 1745,* in favour of the house of Stuart, a great proportion of the people, and in some parts whole districts,† were members of the old Established Church of Scotland—that is, the Episcopal.‡ And when by this political convulsion the body was broken, a faithful few still remained

---

* See Appendix, Note I.

† The Rev. John Skinner, grandfather of the present Bishop Skinner, of Aberdeen, was minister of Longside, in Aberdeenshire, which was chiefly composed of Episcopalians, until the severe penal statutes of 1746, under which Mr. Skinner was imprisoned, and his chapel destroyed. Yet he remained there as the Episcopal clergyman to the end of his long life; and at this day Episcopalians are very numerous in the north of Scotland.

‡ "Here it was that, enjoying the conversation, and the benefit of reading, under the direction of a worthy Episcopal clergyman in that neighbourhood, *he became a convert to the principles of Episcopacy, and united himself to the venerable remains of the old Established Church of Scotland."—Life of the Rev. John Skinner, of Longside.*

true to the Church; and of the Scottish Episcopal Church, so pure and primitive in its discipline, it was pronounced by a venerable bishop of the Church of England, that if St. Paul were to return upon earth, he would most probably live among the Episcopalians of Scotland, as the persons most resembling those to whom he had been accustomed in his former life.*

The Reformed Catholic Church has also sprung up in great vigour, and spreads and flourishes, in the United States of North America.† It has now flung out its wide-spreading branches over the eastern world. Wheresoever the English flag waves, there is planted the standard of the Church. Long may it flourish!

In the modern reformed religious world, therefore, authority and custom and numbers are very much on the side of Episcopacy, as we now style the Catholic and Apostolical government and discipline of

* See Appendix, Note K.
† Whither the first prelate, Bishop Seabury, was sent from the Episcopal Church of Scotland.

the Church of Christ. In the ancient Christian world it was universal, as the name *catholic* signifies. The word *bishop*,* indeed, which now gives it its designation, is, as every tyro in biblical criticism is aware, of the same import, or describes the same person or order, as *presbyter*, in the New Testament. But this does not affect the question of the antiquity of the Church. The Episcopal office is the same as that of the Apostles. Bishops were anciently called Apostles long after the death of the twelve, who were emphatically Apostles, being the eye-witnesses of the majesty of Christ.† The title was, we are told by the ancients, after a time, discontinued, out of reverence to the twelve; and *bishop*, one of the titles of the second order,

---

* Episcopus—ἐπίσκοπος.

† "For we have not followed cunningly-devised fables, when we made known unto you the power and coming of our Lord Jesus Christ, but were EYE-WITNESSES OF HIS MAJESTY." ἐπόπται γενηθέντες τῆς ἐκείνου μεγαλειότητος. 2 Peter i. 16.

These last words are used with reference to the *transfiguration*. *Vide* Bloomfield's Greek Testament in loc.

was substituted in its place.* St. John, moreover, designates the governors of the seven apocalyptic Churches, *angels*, or *messengers*, which is a word of similar import to the word *apostles*.†

In thus deducing the history and the apostolical authority of the bishops and governors of the Church,‡ it follows that the two inferior orders of presbyter and deacon are, as the rubric expresses it, "necessary in the Church of Christ, and also that the people ought to esteem them in their offices." And, in the strong language of the great Apostle of the Gentiles to the Church of Thessalonica, "we beseech you, brethren, to know them that labour among you, and are over you in the Lord, and admonish you; and to esteem them very highly in love for their works' sake."§

* See Ante Note E, where the passage of Theodoret to this effect is cited, and the writers there referred to.

† See Appendix, Note L.
‡ See Appendix, Note M.
§ 1 Thess. v. 12, 13.

The authority of presbyters, or elders, which Paul and Barnabas ordained in every Church they planted, St. Paul, addressing the presbyters of the Church of Ephesus, thus establishes—" Take heed, therefore, unto yourselves, and to all the flock, *over which the Holy Ghost hath made you overseers,* to feed the Church of God, which He hath purchased with His own blood."* Thus presbyters are not appointed by the people, but by the Holy Ghost, and ministerially set apart, or ordained, by the bishop, along with whom, according to ancient usage, and as the rubric of our office appoints, " the priests or presbyters present shall lay their hands severally upon the head of every one that receiveth the order of priesthood."†

In like manner, deacons, to whom some deny any ministerial authority, were set apart by the Holy Ghost, and ordained by the Apostles; and that they were thus

---

* Acts xx. 28.
† See rubric for the ordering of priests.

chosen and appointed for higher offices than to "serve tables," and distribute alms, is evident both from the nature of the thing and the immediate effusion of the Holy Ghost upon Stephen, who, "full of faith and power, did great wonders and miracles among the people," and was the first martyr to the faith. The concurrent history of the Church, from the apostolic age downwards, makes them the third order of the ministry, with authority to baptize, and, by license from the bishop, to preach.* So now persons are *appointed* and ordained by the hands of the bishop *alone,* in strict accordance with the history of the first appointment of deacons in the Acts of the Apostles. "Wherefore, brethren† (said the twelve to the murmuring disciples), look ye out among you seven men of honest report, full of the

---

* See Bingham's Ecclesiastical Antiquities, book xiv., chap. iv., sect. 2; in which the rule of the ancient Church is fully laid down and explained, that "preaching was the proper office of bishops and presbyters, in ordinary cases, and not of deacons."

† Acts vi. 3, 6.

Holy Ghost and wisdom, whom we may appoint over this business." And when they were "set before the Apostles, and they had prayed, they laid their hands on them."

St. Paul, in his Epistles to Timothy, and in his personal charges to that beloved and adopted son, unquestionably refers more immediately to the Episcopal office than to the office of presbyter. Thus in the text, already cited for another purpose at the outset of this discourse, the appeal is personally to him as to the strengthening of divine grace, in order that he might more fitly discharge his official duty as a bishop of the Church of Christ. "Thou, therefore, my son, be strong in the grace that is in Christ Jesus. And the things that thou hast heard of me among many witnesses, the same commit thou to faithful men, who shall be able to teach others also."*

But in the text to this discourse, which

* 2 Tim. ii. 1, 2.

I shall now proceed to examine, the apostolic exhortation applies equally to Timothy the bishop, and to the "faithful men," to whom he should "commit the things that he had heard of" St. Paul "among many witnesses." It applies to the pastoral offices, whether of bishop, the pastor of the entire diocese, the presbyter of presbyters, or to those ordained by him as "overseers" of the flock and presbyters of the Church. It applies likewise to the deacon, who baptizes, and preaches with the license of the bishop. Every one, therefore, who is an authorized, and would be a faithful minister, does the inspired apostle exhort in these words: "Study to show thyself approved unto God, a workman that needeth not to be ashamed, rightly dividing the word of truth."

Each branch of this pregnant sentence would of itself fitly form the subject of a separate discourse. Of the first precept, "Study to show thyself *approved* unto God," the strength lies in the term "approved;" a word, affirmatively and negatively, used by no inspired writer of the New Testament, with one solitary exception,* save by St. Paul.

The only effectual mode of "*showing* ourselves approved unto God" is by *being* so, as far as it is possible for a frail and corrupt creature, such as man, to be "approved" before Him, in whose sight the heavens are not clean, and who charges His angels with folly. This should be the aim and the standard of all professing Christians; how much more so, my reverend brethren, of the ministry? Lowly and humbly to feel

" As ever in our great Taskmaster's eye;"

---

* James i. 12. The allusion is to Ecclesiasticus ii. 5.—" For gold is *tried* in the fire, and acceptable men in the furnace of adversity." ὅτι ἐν πυρὶ δοκιμάζεται χρυσὸς, κ. τ. λ. " Blessed (says St. James) is the man that endureth temptation; for when he is *tried* [or *proved*] ὅτι δόκιμος γενόμενος κ. τ. λ. he shall receive the crown of life, which the Lord hath prepared for them that love Him." St. James refers to the practical fruit, or effects of faith, in the patient endurance of the trials and temptations of life. St. Paul, in the text, " Study to show thyself *approved* unto God," Σπούδασον σεαυτὸν δόκιμον, κ. τ. λ., refers rather to the

As the servants of an omniscient Lord, who knoweth the very thoughts of our hearts; to pray for His grace and guidance in all things; to walk in "the way," of which, by His Holy Spirit, He hath "informed" us, and into which He hath promised to "guide us with His eye;"* this is the rule of that faithful minister who "studies to show himself approved unto God." Our Apostle gives us, elsewhere, a beautiful instance of his own humility, and an awful warning of human instability, when he applies this caution to himself—" I keep under my body, and bring it into subjection; lest that by any means, when I have preached to others, I myself should be a castaway"—a reprobate.†

The grave duty of the faithful minister

---

sound faith, and faithful preaching of the word of God. Both are eminently necessary to the ministers of the Gospel. (*Vide* Schmid's Greek Concordance in voc. δόκιμος and ἀδόκιμος).

* Psalm xxxii. 9.

† Μήπως ἄλλοις κηρύξας αὐτὸς ἀδόκιμος γένωμαι. 1 Cor. ix. 27.

is plainly to "study to show himself approved unto God" in sound doctrine, and a pure and holy life; to "hold fast the form of sound words,"* delivered by Christ and his Apostles, "in faith and love which is in Christ Jesus;" and, in the words of an expositor, not of our Church, but an ornament to any community, "to endeavour so to cultivate and improve the heart and mind, that he may not be a reproach to Him from whom he professed to receive his commission."†

The faithful minister must, moreover, be "a workman that needeth not be ashamed." THE SINGLE EYE in all things; simplicity of heart and purity of life; the "virtue," or moral courage,‡ which, according to

---

* 2 Tim. i. 13. † Dr. Adam Clarke.

‡ Ἀρετή. 2 Pet. i. 5. I give but *one* sense of this word. *Military* courage is its first sense, being derived from Ἄρης *Mars*, the supposed god of war (see Parkhurst in voc). It is hence defined by Joseph Planche, in his Dictionnaire Grec. Francois, compiled from Stephen's "Thesaurus," in these graduated senses: "vertu guerriere, vigueur, la vertu, *dans un sens genérique*." Schleusner, in voc. ἀρετή, defines it yet more generally. But the theological student

St. Peter, must always be the attendant upon faith; sincerity and ingenuousness; and conscientiousness and inflexible integrity—these are the principles and these are the virtues which, by the grace of God, will effectually shield the minister of Christ from the justly reprobated character of " a workman that needeth *be* ashamed."

The last requisite of a faithful minister of his Divine Master is that upon which all the rest depend, as based on a solid foundation, like the house of the wise man upon a rock, which neither the violence of the elements of nature, nor " the craft and subtilty of the devil or man," can overthrow: this is " rightly dividing the word of truth."

The original word for "rightly dividing" is a sacrificial term;* it refers to the

---

is referred to a very able note on the entire passage in Bloomfield's Greek Testament—the best work for students which has yet appeared.

* Ὀρθοτομοῦντα. See an excellent critical note on this phrase in Bloomfield's Greek Testament on this place. See likewise Whitby's and Dr. Adam Clarke's "rightly dividing" of the sacrifice which was to be laid upon the altar. As some parts, not to be offered, were separated from those that were offered; so does the Apostle require Timothy, and after him every faithful preacher of "the word of truth," to separate from it all false and pernicious doctrines and systems of men, all noxious and idle controversies, "foolish and unlearned questions gendering strife,"* all superfluous and unnecessary opinions and things; and to give his hearers the unadulterated and "sincere milk of the word."†

This is the most ancient, the most common, and it appears, on the whole, the most correct and consistent exposition of this

---

Commentaries. "By *rightly dividing the word of truth* we are to understand his continuing in the true doctrine, and teaching *that* to every person; and, according to our Lord's simile, *giving each his portion of meat in due season—milk to babes, strong meat to the full grown, comfort* to the *disconsolate, reproof* to the *irregular* and *careless;* and, in a word, finding out the necessities of his hearers, and preaching so as to meet those necessities."—*Dr. Adam Clarke.*

* 2 Tim. ii. 23. † See Whitby.

striking phrase.* And surely a more wise and a more salutary admonition was never, and could never, be given for the guidance of "faithful men, who shall be able (and authorized) to teach others." We learn from the inspired records of the New Testament, the writings of St. Paul himself at the conclusion of this Epistle, and from the Catholic Epistles of St. Peter and St. Jude, how, in the apostolic age, Gnostics, and other false teachers, adulterated the pure waters of the fountain of life and immortality, by *not* "rightly dividing the word of truth." "Now as Jannes and Jambres withstood Moses, so did these also resist the truth: men of corrupt minds, *reprobate*† *concerning the faith.*"

St. Peter does, indeed, allow that in the

---

* The learned reader may also consult Parkhurst in voc. ὀρθοτόμεω.

† 2 Tim. iii. 8. Ἀδόκιμοι περὶ τὴν πίστιν. Ἀδόκιμος " properly signifies *reprobus, rejectaneus,* as used of *bad money,* which, as it will not pass, is *good for nothing.* Thus (by the same metaphor as in our word *naughty*) it comes to mean what is, in every sense, bad."—*Bloomfield's Greek Testament,* in Rom. i. 28.

Epistles of " his beloved brother Paul are some things hard to be understood, which they that are unlearned and unstable, wrest, as they do also the other Scriptures, unto their own destruction."* These respected the end of the world, concerning which there were various foolish and pernicious speculations in the time of the Apostles. But all Scripture is liable to be, and constantly is, " wrested, by unlearned and unstable" men, to their own destruction, and to that of others : and the ministers of God are those "faithful men" to whom the " word of truth" is delivered as a precious deposit, and of which they are the guardians and protectors. They must, therefore, "*study* rightly to divide the word of truth."

St. James, and certainly St. John, especially in his Gospel, appear to have written their noble and beautiful Scriptures for the correction of heresy and error, doctrinal and practical. St. John's Gospel, it is the

---

* 2 Peter iii. 15, 16.

concurrent voice of antiquity, was composed by the special desire of the Bishops of Asia, against Cerinthus and other heretics, especially against the dogmas of the Ebionites, then springing up, *who denied* Christ *to have come in the flesh*. This beautiful evangelist, we are told, was compelled by almost all the Bishops of Asia, and by deputations from many Churches, to write more fully of our Saviour's divinity. And ecclesiastical history informs us, that when he was thus urged by the brethren to write, he answered that he would, provided that they would all join in prayer and fasting to God; which being done, and *he being fully inspired*, he burst forth in that divine preface, " In the beginning was the word,* and the word was with God, and the word was God."†

---

* Always translated by Dr. Hales " the oracle;" but by Lardner, from whom Hales takes the passage, it is as in our version, " the word."

† Lardner's Works, vol. v., p. 40, 35. Dr. Hales's Analysis of Chronology, &c., vol. iii., p. 23, 24. Second edition, 8vo. London, 1830.

And do not we, my brethren, live in "perilous times," when "men are lovers of their own selves, covetous, boasters, proud, blasphemers, disobedient to parents, unthankful, unholy; lovers of pleasure more than lovers of God; having a form of godliness, but denying the power thereof?"* Is not this all-improving and vaunted enlightened age the very image and reflection of the times of our great and noble-minded Apostle, when men were "ever learning, but never able to come to the knowledge of the truth?"† When, on the contrary, they did also, as now, "resist the truth; men of corrupt minds, reprobate concerning the faith?"

Are not these, moreover, I ask, in the language of another Apostle, the times when there are "false teachers among us, who privily," nay, openly "bring in damnable heresies, even denying the Lord that bought them, and bring upon themselves swift destruction?" Against such awful

---

* 2 Tim. iii. 1, 2, 4, .5 † 2 Tim. iii. 7, 8.

heretics as these was the divine Gospel of St. John sent forth, winged with the prayers and watered with the tears of the Church. Against such heretics at various subsequent ages of the Church, when the mantle of inspiration and prophecy was dropped on no surviving believers, THE CHURCH has opposed, by the authority of Christ and the presence of His Spirit, "alway, even unto the end of the world," such documents as the Nicene and Athanasian creeds. Against such heretics have the bishops and presbyters of our own venerable Church resolutely fought with "the sword of the Spirit, which is the WORD OF GOD." Need I mention?—yes, I will mention, for our encouragement, my reverend brethren, such eminent names as Bishops Bull, Horsley,* Magee, and the

---

* *Fas est ab hoste doceri.* Gibbon, the historian, in the memoirs of his life and writings, when touching upon the correspondence between Priestly and himself, thus pays the highest and justly merited compliment to Bishop Horsley's noble work against this heresiarch. "*From my replies,* he (Priestly) has nothing to hope or fear; but *his Socinian shield has*

first and the greatest glory of Christian India, Bishop Middleton.* Need I mention the renowned presbyters of the Church of England, in the ranks of this army of saints and godly leaders? Who will not remember the names of Leslie, Barrow, Nares, and a host of writers who in past time have risen, and are constantly rising, to oppose these " damnable heresies?"

And how, my brethren, have these "faithful men," and "good soldiers of our Lord Jesus Christ," combated the leviathan of infidelity and heresy? By "rightly dividing the word of truth"—by devoting all the best part of their lives—all the purest and strongest energies of the mind, heart, and spirit to the study of the inspired

---

repeatedly been pierced by the mighty spear of Horsley."—*Gibbon's Miscellaneous Works,* vol. i., p. 232. Octavo edition.

* See Appendix, Note N. To the list both of bishops and presbyters I might add many more. I cannot but name two presbyters, Mr. Jones of Nayland, whose "Doctrine of the Trinity" preserves many souls in the faith; and the historian of Manchester, Whitaker's very able and learned work, "The Origin of Arianism disclosed," published in 1791, and dedicated to Bishop Horsley.

Scriptures. By calling in all legitimate aid to carry on this heavenly warfare with the spirits of darkness;* whether to cloud the understanding, to corrupt the heart, or to depress the spirit, be the object of this hateful and infernal host. By laying aside all worldly and secular thoughts, and all ambitious desires of personal aggrandisement, or personal interest and gratification, most unbecoming the faithful minister and " the good soldier of Jesus Christ." For what says our Apostle? " No man that warreth entangleth himself with the affairs of this life; that he may please Him who hath chosen him to be a soldier. And if a man also strive for masteries, yet is he not crowned, except he strive lawfully. The husbandman that

* " The country parson is full of all knowledge. They say it is an ill mason that refuseth any stone: and there is no knowledge, but, in a skilful hand, serves either positively as it is, or else to illustrate some other knowledge. But the chief and top of his knowledge consists in the book of books, the storehouse and magazine of life and comfort—the holy Scriptures. There he sucks and lives."—*Herbert's Country Parson.*

laboureth must be first partaker of the fruits. Remember (concludes the dying Apostle, for this Epistle was written just before his martyrdom) what I say; and the Lord give thee"—may the Lord give us, my brethren—" understanding in all things."*

These deadly heresies take their rise from almost imperceptible sources. Every departure from sound doctrine and sober discipline is the first budding of the poison tree of heresy. Hence the wise fathers of our Church, in the ordination service of priests, which you will presently hear—and I pray God that none may hear it without emotions of reverence towards God and His Church—after the priest is solemnly asked by the bishop whether he think that he is truly called to the Church, and will instruct the people out of the Scriptures, and administer the doctrine and sacraments, the bishop puts this question—" Will you be ready, with all faithful diligence, to banish and drive away all errone-

* 2 Tim. ii. 3-7.

ous and strange doctrine, contrary to God's word?" And again—"Will you be diligent in prayers, and in reading of the Holy Scriptures, and in such studies as help to the knowledge of the same, laying aside the world and the flesh?"

After such solemn and awful vows, which are bound upon every presbyter of the Church, who will have the hardihood to affirm that the faithful minister acts contrary to his duty—this "woe being unto him if he preach not the Gospel"*— when he does his utmost to oppose, to banish and drive away all erroneous and strange doctrine," which he believes to be "contrary to God's word," by every lawful means in his power? This most important duty, though it be discharged with unshrinking firmness, and, if need be, in the face of the world, must yet be done without strife, and with as much gentleness as possible. We must, my brethren,

* "For necessity is laid upon me; yea, woe is unto me if I preach not the Gospel." 1 Cor. ix. 16.

"study to show ourselves approved in the sight of God," by its plainly appearing to MAN that we do it as an act of duty, without favour or affection, and without the slightest personal resentment against those whom it is our bounden duty to exhort, and even to reprove. For this, too, our great and wise Apostle has given us a guide. "The servant of the Lord must not strive; but be gentle unto all men, apt to teach, patient, in meekness instructing those that oppose themselves."* The priest, therefore, undertakes, before his bishop, to "maintain and set forward, as much as lieth in him, quietness, peace, and love, among all Christian people, and especially among them that are, or shall be, committed to his charge."

Allow me to add a few words respecting errors in doctrine and discipline, which, although in this day considered venial, will nevertheless lead now, as in all foregone time, to the like fatal results. For

* 2 Tim. ii. 24, 25.

truth is eternal—it is of no time—it is governed by its own immutable laws. We have seen how, from small beginnings, the most dangerous errors in doctrine, called by the Apostle " damnable heresies," crept into the Church in the apostolic age; until, before the destruction of Jerusalem, to which period it is supposed the sacred writers allude by " the last times," heresy had grown to such a monstrous height, that men " denied the Lord that bought them." Against these heretics, we have seen, St. John, who survived the destruction of Jerusalem, wrote his inestimable Gospel, which by some learned men is supposed to be the last of his compositions.

In the age we live in, alas! have we not likewise many who deny the divinity of the Saviour, and glory in their proud and perilous apostasy? Such are in our own country; but they are not, blessed be God, within the bosom of our Apostolic Church. Such heretics cut themselves off from us by their apostasy.* But let us, for one moment, cast our eyes around the Christian world, especially and solely on those Churches and communities which left the Romish or Western Church in the sixteenth century. And what Church or Establishment (with, perhaps, the exception of the Lutheran Churches of Denmark, Norway, and Sweden, of which little is certainly known, save that they are Episcopal†)—what Church, as an Establishment, save our own,‡ is sound in the faith? The Church of Prussia is, by the testimony of intelligent travellers,§ outwardly in a degraded state.

* Allusion is here specially intended to the clergy, and the religious portion of the community—individuals who "care for none of these things," and may formally attend our ministrations, do not affect the question. None can *use* the Prayer Book, as an office of devotion, who is a Socinian, or a modern Unitarian. A clergyman is self-condemned by such heterodoxy; and if he do not depart from the Church, of which he is an unworthy minister, his superior, as in a recent case in the diocese of Exeter, must and will apply his authority to expel him.
 † See Ante-note H, in the Appendix.
 ‡ See Appendix, Note O.
 § See Appendix, Note P.

The clergy are held in no repute; religion, therefore, can have no value in the eyes of the people. But look at Germany generally, of which Prussia, though a separate kingdom, may in this respect be considered a part. Are not Socinianism, Unitarianism, and what, in this country, is now known by the denomination of NEOLOGY, all, in various forms, denying the Lord that bought them, and especially the inspiration of the Scriptures? Are not these the prevailing opinions and dogmas respecting the Christian religion in that first region of the Reformed faith?* Is Holland†, one of the Calvinistic countries, much sounder in the faith? And whence hath the blast of infidelity gone forth with a more withering sound than from the metaphysicians and literary men of Presbyterian Scotland?‡ But look at Ge-

* See Appendix, Note Q.

† Respecting Holland, I have not met with any books which confirm this; but I have heard travellers, who have been in Holland, assert that great laxity of religious opinion prevails in that country.

‡ See Appendix, Note R.

neva—once the glory of a not inconsiderable portion of professsors of the Reformed faith. Here was a sect, or society, formed into a national establishment by the great Calvin himself, in many respects as a divine, and in all respects, personally, a holy and a venerable man; perhaps the most intellectual, and certainly the most metaphysical, of the Reformers; but, alas! the greatest innovator.* Geneva is now a Socinian establishment!!! †

And if it be enquired how these Churches and communities thus fatally erred, and fell from the truth as it is in Jesus, must we not reply, according to the immutable laws of truth, that their fall was occasioned equally by errors in doctrine and in discipline? Great as were those justly eminent Reformers, Luther and Calvin, both, but especially Calvin, erred in the doctrine of predestination.‡ They and their followers, with few exceptions, threw off

---

* See Appendix, Note S. † See Appendix, Note T.
‡ See Appendix, note. U.

the apostolical government of the Church of Christ.

Let us, then, my brethren, while we mourn over the errors of such mighty men, and of our brethren who have been followers of their errors, rather than of their bright and illustrious virtues—let us bless God, that, by His gracious and divine providence, our lot has fallen in more pleasant and more secure places; and that we belong to a Church, primitive in its government and discipline, and pure in its doctrine, of which you, my brethren, who are candidates for ordination, will be ordained ministers this day.

"Study, therefore, to show yourselves approved unto God, workmen that need not be ashamed, rightly dividing the word of truth. But shun profane and vain babblings, for they will increase unto more ungodliness. Foolish and unlearned questions avoid, knowing that they do but gender strifes."* But study the inspired

* 2 Tim. ii. 15, 16, 23.

and "holy Scriptures, which are able to make you wise unto salvation, through faith which is in Christ Jesus."*

I have already detained you so long, that I have left scarcely any time to address my brethren who will this day be more solemnly enlisted among the soldiers of Christ. But I must be allowed to say a few words of earnest and affectionate exhortation, if I may be permitted so to style it.

You have doubtless, my brethren, heard much that is familiar to you respecting the doctrine and discipline of that Church, of which some of you will be first admitted ministers, as deacons, and others of you will be invested with the higher and much more grave and responsible order of presbyters, or priests. Although you have not the advantage of English students† (but I

* 2 Tim. iii. 15.

† I had hoped to have been able to state that the *Heber Fund*, out of which native students shall be sent to Bishop's College, Calcutta, had been revived and extended in its operations. I regret that this

trust, ere long, that this advantage will be extended to all native students, as it has been to some of my ordained brethren among you), you have read enough to be familiar with the chief features of what I have already said from this place. To this, therefore, I need add nothing.

But there are a few topics on which I should wish to say a very few words.

To you, who are to be made deacons, I fear I can offer little or no advice which can serve for your guidance, save what is very general. You are to discharge the important office of missionaries to your own people. I am not myself a missionary, and am therefore very incompetent to speak to you on the subject. Thus far I may say—your office is of the last importance to your own salvation, and perhaps to thousands of your own countrymen and countrywomen, who are yet immersed in heathen darkness and corruption, or who

---

"consummation," however "devoutly to be wished," is not yet attained; but I trust that either *that*, or some other, will soon be in operation.

have but just emerged, and that very imperfectly, from the shadow of death.

You have, I am aware, served for some years as catechists among your people. You now go to them in another and a more sacred character—you will go to them invested with the authority of deacons of the Church of Christ. It is the same office, you will bear in mind, which was held by St. Stephen, the proto-martyr of the faith—the first saint who shed his blood, and thus bore *witness*, hence called a *martyr*, to the death and resurrection of Jesus Christ, and thus testified his faith in the SAVIOUR of the world. The same holy office, or order, was also sustained by Philip, who, on "the scattering abroad" of the disciples on the death of St. Stephen and the persecutions of Saul (afterwards Paul, himself miraculously converted no long time subsequently), "went down into the city of Samaria, and preached Christ unto them" who dwelt in that city with the greatest success. The same Philip afterwards converted and baptized "a man of Ethiopia, an eunuch of great authority under Candace, queen of the Ethiopians."*

An office held by such distinguished saints—one the very first martyr to the faith, and the other a missionary, as you are—such an office is, doubtless, one of great and awful importance. You should, therefore, my brethren, think of the great things achieved by these holy men, and of their deep humility. Great things like these it is not to be supposed you will be called upon to do, or to sustain. But what you have to do is in itself great beyond all comparison. It is to convert the heathen and the idolator; to bring him from darkness into the kingdom of light; and to keep him in that holy way of salvation, into which, by God's grace, you shall have turned his feet.

Habitual prayer, humility of mind, a deep internal reverence, and a continual study of the holy Scriptures—these are

* Acts viii. 4, 5, 25-27.

habiliments with which you must henceforth invest your souls. You must not be carried away with the notion that you are elevated in the world. On the contrary, as we have already heard from the great Apostle himself, "the good soldier of Christ doth not entangle himself with the affairs of this life." This humble and holy Apostle wrote these words and this Epistle just before he himself suffered martyrdom under the execrable tyrant, Nero, emperor of Rome. This was the end and consummation of all the labours and sorrows of this mighty Apostle. It was his glory, and his "exceeding great reward." But St. Stephen, the deacon, was the first martyr. St. Philip, the deacon, the holy Apostles, and the first preachers of the Gospel, were missionaries to the heathen. Suffering and persecution awaited them whithersoever they went. Such may be your lot. Be therefore faithful men, and "good soldiers of Jesus Christ. Study to show yourselves approved unto God, workmen that need not be ashamed, rightly dividing the word of truth."

To you, my brethren, who for some years* have borne the office of deacons, and are now to be invested with the office and order of priesthood, my limits will allow me to say very little. Your duties and your situation are difficult. Some of your difficulties I do perhaps know better than those of our brethren, the missionaries.† There is, however, one caution that I gave to them which is perhaps even *more* necessary for your guidance. This is, that with your new and higher office of presbyter, or priest, you increase in lowliness and humility of heart and of deportment. I feel persuaded, my brethren, that you will forgive my saying so much on this head; I do it in all kindness and simplicity. You have to minister among

---

* See Appendix, Note V.
† Two candidates for priesthood were the Rev. Mr. Arndt and the Rev. Mr. Ondatjie, the Portuguese and Malabar chaplains. The two deacons were native Singhalese, employed in the Church mission at Cotta.

those who have known you in situations of less importance; lower in the conventional scale of society; and in all things different from that holy and important station and office you will presently hold, as presbyters of the Church of England. If He, who knew what was in man, who needed not that any one should tell Him, who read the heart, being God and man—if He, our Divine Redeemer, was rejected of His own countrymen, and held in suspicion and distrust by His family and relatives, because, as He told them, "a prophet was not without honour, save in his own country"—surely any one of us, on a change of our circumstances and situation of life, may well be warned, and will do wisely, to walk with the greatest care and circumspection. Your responsibility, my brethren, is greatly and awfully increased. Let the sense of this deepened responsibility, I beseech you, rest in your minds and hearts, as faithful men and ministers, into whose keeping will be committed the sacred and awful charge of the salvation of souls, when you are ordained to the office of presbyters of the Church of Christ.*

In other respects, I need offer no further advice, save that, according to your vows, you will be diligent in "reading of the holy Scriptures, and in such studies as help to the knowledge of them;" remembering that the day of our ordination is the beginning of our labours and of our more intense study of the way of salvation, in holy writ, to the end of our lives.†

Let us all, therefore, my reverend brethren, " read, mark, learn, and inwardly digest" the word of God. Let us particularly study St. Paul's Epistles to Timothy, the inspired manuals of Churchmen, especially his second and last, which is, perhaps, the most affecting composition to

---

* See Appendix, Note W. This Note applies equally, and perhaps more strongly, to the other candidates, the deacons, who are missionaries to the natives, their countrymen.

† See Appendix, Note X.

be found even among the writings of this mighty Apostle. It was his last Epistle. It was written, as it were, with his blood.

Let us, my brethren, guided by this holy and wise Apostle, as faithful ministers of the Gospel of Christ, "study to show ourselves approved unto God, workmen that need not be ashamed, rightly dividing the word of truth." For "all Scripture is given by inspiration of God, and is profitable for doctrine, for reproof, for correction, for instruction in righteousness; that the man of God may be perfect, thoroughly furnished unto all good works;"* and that we may all, both pastors and our flocks, daily "grow in grace, and in the knowledge of our Lord and Saviour Jesus Christ. To Him be glory both now and for ever. Amen."†

* 2 Tim. iii. 16, 17. † 2 Pet. iii. 18.

APPENDIX.

Και οι αποστολοι ημων εγνωσαν δια του κυριου ημων Ιησου Χριστου, ὁτι ερις εσται επι του ονοματος τῆς επισκοπης· δια ταυτην ουν την αιτιαν, προγνωσιν ειληφοτες τελειαν, κατεστησαν τους προειρημενους, και μεταξυ επινομην δεδωκασιν, ὁπως, εαν κοιμηθωσιν, διαδεξωνται ἑτεροι διεδοκιμασμενοι ανδρες την λειτουργιαν αυτων. Τους ουν κατασταθεντας ὑπ' εκεινων, η μεταξυ ὑφ' ἑτερων ελλογιμων ανδρων συνευδοκησασης της εκκλησιας πασης, - - - τουτους ου δικαιως νομιζομεν αποβαλεσθαι της λειτουργιας. *S. Clementis ad Corinthios. Epist. I. Sect. xliv.*

"So likewise our Apostles knew by our Lord Jesus Christ, that contentions would arise on account of the ministry [or, 'about the name of the bishopric']. And therefore, having a perfect foreknowledge of this, they appointed persons, as we have before said, and then gave directions how, when they should die, other chosen and approved men should succeed in their ministry [or, 'left a list of other chosen and approved persons who should succeed them in their ministry']. Wherefore we cannot think that those may justly be thrown out of their ministry, who were either appointed by them, or afterwards chosen by other eminent men, WITH THE CONSENT OF THE WHOLE CHURCH."

PREFACE TO APPENDIX.

Three years and upwards have elapsed since the date of the publication of the Sermon, to which the following pages are an Appendix. It seems, therefore, proper to explain why it was not at first attached to the Sermon, and why, at so distant a date, it now appears in this form.

The Author consented to the publication of the Sermon upon the understanding that he should subjoin an Appendix. Many important subjects were briefly stated, and others but barely touched upon, which seemed to demand a more extended verification than could be made in a discourse from the pulpit. It was, therefore, stated in the Dedication, that " he had laid down certain principles, for which some readers might require proof. He had asserted some important facts, which by others might be thought to demand illustration. A concise statement and a condensed argument are enough for clergymen. The subjects of their studies and their habits of thought, render it easy to fill up the outline. The public had a right to demand something more demonstrative. He had, therefore, in the Appendix, endeavoured to throw together such facts and other illustrations as bear upon the subject-matter of the discourse."

Such evidences and illustrations necessarily consist, for the most part, of copious citations from various authors, along with other matter. The additional expense of printing was, at the time, deemed sufficient to render it inexpedient to publish the Appendix along with the Sermon; and a notice was subjoined, "that the Appendix would *shortly* be published in a separate form."

No steps were, however, taken towards this publication; and the manuscript copy lay in the printer's hands at Madras, until, at the latter end of 1842, it was recovered by the author. He had abandoned the purpose of printing it. But upon an attentive perusal of the papers, after they had been so long out of his hands, he still thought that possibly they might be useful to the members of the Church in this colony, where publications of the kind are "far and few." He has therefore redeemed his pledge, though not without considerable diffidence, and presents the following sheets, more particularly for the use of the younger members of the Church of England.

One advantage will accrue from this late publication. Much discussion on Church discipline and doctrine has issued from the press in England since the beginning of the year 1840, when the Sermon was printed. Some extracts from a few of these publicatons will be found in a SUPPLEMENT.

The Author had proposed to himself, as an Introduction, to collate the primitive apostolical Fathers who were contemporary with and immediately succeeded the Apostles; and from their writings, especially those of St. Clement and St. Ignatius, to adduce testimonies of that apostolic form of Church government—the threefold ministry of bishops, priests, and deacons—which, from the days of the Apostles to the Reformation of the Western Church, fifteen hundred years, has been *uninterruptedly* maintained, and, with comparatively small exception, to the present day is, and to the day of judgment will be, maintained by the Christian world. But this purpose is relinquished, though considerable collections were made. It is not the intention of this publication to excite controversy with other churches and communities, or with respectable and conscientious Christians who are in separation from the Church of England; but it is the Author's wish to instruct those members of his own Church who have not sufficiently enquired into the subjects of these sheets; to warn the unwary and unstable of the danger incurred by abandoning the visible Church of Christ, into which they have been baptized; and to incite all to enquire for themselves, with sobriety and humility of mind.

This is an age, however, when Churchmen—especially the clergy, whose solemn duty it is to watch over the flock—should not be timid or backward, on all fitting occasions, openly to avow and boldly to maintain their principles—those principles which they believe to have sustained apostles and apostolic men through sorrows and dangers, through persecutions and martyrdoms, and which will support all sincere Christians, if honestly and consistently carried out in their lives and conversations, through all trials and temptations. When these genuine results of a pure faith do not appear, it is not from any lack of soundness in the principles of faith, but from a failure in the means of maintaining them. Were the primitive discipline of the Church now enforced, and the Church itself supported by the State and by the people, as we read in the earlier and purer ages of Christianity; were bishops planted much more thickly, and the numbers of the inferior clergy proportionately augmented, in the Church of England and Ireland, in the mother country and in the colonies, discipline would be enforced in its ancient strictness; and " the truth as it is in Jesus—the faith once delivered to the saints," would be widely proclaimed and carefully inculcated in its primitive purity.

But while every Churchman should firmly and unflinchingly assert his principles, as a member of any pure branch—whether in England, Scotland, or America, and the numerous colonial possessions of Great Britain and Ireland—of what he believes and knows to be THE CATHOLIC CHURCH OF CHRIST, it follows not that he should be intolerant of other pious men who honestly and conscientiously differ from him—and, least of all, that he should deny salvation to others, whether communities or individuals; though he may perceive that they are exposed to greater dangers than they would have been exposed to in the Church.

The strong bond of unity among Christians, and that which emphatically constitutes the unity of the Church, is, in its most comprehensive sense, CHARITY. It unites us in the bonds of one common faith and love to each other. It is the only effectual means of reconciling ourselves to differences, and to be loving and tolerant to the persons of those who stand without the pale of the communion of the Church—though, as we must believe, on mistaken principles, yet on the ground of conscience. That it is the purpose of the Divine will that all who believe in Christ should be of one communion—in the strictest sense, "one fold under one shepherd"

—we cannot doubt. It is the SIN OF MAN which in this, as in other instances, defeats his own happiness, by not fulfilling the will of God; *not the sin of the* INDIVIDUAL—for there may be, and doubtless there are, cases where, under the peculiar circumstances, *individuals* are most safe without the pale of the Church, provided that they hold the fundamental verities. They are undoubtedly subject to many hindrances and inconveniences, from which they would have been protected in the Church. But the sin of placing them where they are is not *their sin.* IT IS THE SIN OF MAN GENERALLY: his headstrong will sets itself against the will of God.

All that is left, therefore, for Churchmen, in the present state of things, is, as respects themselves, to obey the apostolic injunction, " with all lowliness and meekness, with long-suffering, forbearing one another in love; endeavouring to keep the unity of the spirit in the bond of peace;" and to feel and to live in peace and charity with those who are not of their communion, without in any respect compromising their own principles. They will thus command the respect and conciliate the affection of all men.

If any man should be tolerant of the opinions of others, so long as they do not *vitally* fall from the faith—and then a Christian love must be shown to their souls in gaining them over to the truth—it is THE CHURCHMAN. This toleration is perfectly distinct and differen' from the spurious *liberalism* of the day, which is tolerant only of the opinions of others respecting the religion of Christ, because, like Gallio, "they care for none of these things."

But a true Churchman stands upon a lofty eminence, equally as respects doctrine and discipline. Deep sorrow indeed he must feel for those who consistently infringe upon the unity of the Church. But if he be well versed in the Scriptures; if he be correctly informed and instructed in the history and constitution of the Church, "built upon the foundation of the Apostles and Prophets, Jesus Christ Himself being the chief corner-stone;" if he be as one "who bringeth out of his treasure things new and old;" if, above all, he have particularly learned the apostolic precept, "to forbear one another in love"—such an one possesses in his own bosom all the elements of real toleration and Christian charity. Imperfect information and a weak mind, as well as uncharitableness and a corrupt heart, are ever to be expected in an intolerant Christian. The intolerance of Churchmen, however frequently the character may be and is imputed to them, is, the writer maintains, one of the many and most unjust imputations upon the clergy of the Church of England, as a body; who, "as far as lieth in them, live peaceably with all men," and "endeavour to keep the unity of the spirit in the bond of peace."

Colombo, May, 1843.

APPENDIX.

Note A, Page 22

APOSTOLICAL SUCCESSION.

"The 'many witnesses' (2 Tim. ii. 2) it has been thought best to understand the presbyters and others of the congregation present at Timothy's ordination (mentioned at 1 Tim. i. 18, iv. 14, vi. 12; and 2 Tim. i. 6), which was probably accompanied by a public charge, the substance whereof St. Paul desires may be delivered to others also. The words $\pi\iota\sigma\tau\text{o}\iota\varsigma$—$\delta\iota\delta\alpha\xi\alpha\iota$, advert to the two principal qualifications for the ministry—*fidelity*, and *fitness for preaching or instructing*."—*Bloomfield's Greek Testament*, vol. ii., p. 399, second edition.

"That *depositum* (ch. i. 14) which I committed to thee in the public assembly at thine ordination, do thou also, in like manner, deposit with other faithful men, that the truth may be continued in an uninterrupted succession of such persons."—*Obadiah Walker.*

" The things agreed on, and consented to by all the other Apostles, do thou commit to able men, and appoint them as bishops of the several Churches under thee."—*Dr. Hammond.*

Whitby thinks there is no foundation for all this in the text; but he allows that

" There was also a παρακαταθηκη,* or *depositum* of Christian doctrine delivered to them, who were to preach and instruct others in the faith, and which he commands Timothy to keep (1 Tim. vi. 20, 21), as being entrusted with it, in opposition to those who had erred from the faith, which he calls *the form of sound words which he had been taught,* and which he was to keep in *faith,* and *love* of the *truth* (2 Tim. i. 13), and *that good thing committed to him* (ver. 14) which he was to *keep by the Holy Ghost,* the Spirit which leadeth into all truth, the unction which taught them all things belonging to their office (1 John ii. 20, 27)—the things *in which he was to continue, knowing of*

---

* So in Whitby. The correct and restored reading is παραθηκην. *Vide* Wetsen et a.

whom he had learned them (2 Tim. iii. 14). I lastly grant that all the Fathers, from Irenæus downwards, speak of such a symbol of faith delivered to the Church by the Apostles and their disciples, which the Church received from them, and distributed to her sons, being the one and the same faith which the Church retained throughout the world; than which they believed neither less nor more, and which, for substance, was the same with the Apostles' Creed."— *Whitby on* 2 *Tim.* ii. 2. See also *Lardner's Supplement to the Credibility of the Gospel*, ch. iv., sect. 1. Works, vol. v., p. 284: new edition, in 10 vols.

Dr. Adam Clarke—contrary to the usual fairness of his candid mind and his known love of the Church of England—impugns the doctrine of apostolical succession with great superciliousness, in his comment on this passage of the Apostle to Timothy. (2 Tim. ii. 2.)

" Where (he asks) is the *uninterrupted* apostolical succession? Who can tell? Probably it does not exist on the face of the world. All the pretensions to it by certain Churches are as stupid as they are idle and futile. He who appeals to this for his authority as a Christian minister had best sit down till he has made it out; and this will be done by the next Greek kalends."

This almost sectarian dogmatism, for he was no sectary in his heart, is unworthy so good a man as Dr. Adam Clarke, for whose memory, though I did not know him personally, I entertain both respect and affection. He had few hurtful prejudices while he lived, and he is now in a world where *all* prejudice is wiped away: he lives with the sainted spirits of bishops and presbyters of the Catholic Church. No man, while living, had a more deep and extended faith; and we may now ask, though not of him, why he should demand a mathematical or arithmetical demonstration of a truth, of which the *moral certainty* is arrived at by another and equally satisfactory process. The continuance of this apostolical form of government in the Church, of which we find the foundations and beginnings of the structure clearly defined in the Scriptures of the New Testament, for fifteen hundred years, without interruption, and which still subsists in our own and a few other Reformed Churches — all this abundantly demonstrates the truth of Episcopacy and the apostolical succession. Further, let this be tried by the four rules of the well-known method of the learned and acute Charles Leslie, and this apostolical succession, and other verities of the Episcopal government of the Church, need no further demonstration.

"The rules are these—first, that the matter of fact be such, as that men's outward senses, their eyes and ears, may be judges of it; secondly, that it be done publicly in the face of the world; thirdly, that not only public monuments be kept up in memory of it, but some outward actions to be performed; fourthly, that such monuments and such actions or observances be instituted, and do commence from the time that the matter of fact was done."—*Leslie on Deism.*

Of Episcopacy, I extract from this writer the following passage:—

"But further, Sir, in your search after a Church, you must not only consider the doctrine, but the government—that is, as I said before, you must consider the Church not only as a sect, but as a society; for though every society, founded upon the belief of such tenets, may be called a sect, yet every sect is not a society: and a government cannot be without governors. The Apostles were instituted by Christ the first governors of His Church; and with them and their successors He has promised to be to the end of the world. The Apostles did ordain bishops and governors in all the Churches which they planted throughout the whole world; and these bishops were esteemed the successors of the Apostles, each in his own Church, from the beginning to this day. This was the current notion and language of antiquity—*Omnes Apostolorum successores sunt*—that all bishops were the successors of the Apostles, as St. Jerome speaks *(Epist. ad Evagr.)*; and St. Ignatius, who was constituted, by the Apostles, Bishop of Antioch, salutes the Church of the Trallians—Εν τῳ πληρωματι εν Αποστολικῳ χαρακτηρι—*In the plenitude of the Apostolical character.* Thus it continued from the days of the Apostles to those of John Calvin; in all which time there was not any one Church in the whole Christian world that was not Episcopal. But now it is said by our Dissenters, that there is no need of succession from the Apostles, or those bishops instituted by them; that they can make governors over themselves whom they list; and what signifies the government of the Church, so the doctrine be pure? But this totally dissolves the Church as a society, the government of which consists in the right and title of the governor. And as the Apostle says—'No man taketh this honour to himself, but he that was called of God, as was Aaron.' (Heb. v. 4). And the dispute betwixt him and Korah was not as to any point either of doctrine or worship, but merely upon that of Church government. And St. Jude (ver. 11) brings down the same case to that of the Church; and reason carries it as to all societies. They who will not obey the lawful governor, but set up another in opposition to him, are no longer of the society, but enemies to it, and justly forfeit all the rights and privileges of it."—*Letter from the Author of the Short Method with the Deists*, sect. xiii.

And he concludes with this "infallible demonstration of Episcopacy":—

" For which this is to be said, that it has all the four marks before mentioned, to ascertain any fact, in the concurrent testimony of all Churches, at all times; and therefore must infallibly be the government which the Apostles left upon earth. To which we must adhere till a greater authority than theirs shall alter it.

" I doubt not but all this will determine you to the Church of England, and keep you firm to Episcopacy, as a matter not indifferent.

" And I pray God, that ' He, who hath begun a good work in you, may perfect it until the day of Jesus Christ. Amen.' "—*Ibid.*, sect. xiv.

Prejudice, rather than demonstrative reasoning, is opposed to the Church.

" The difficulty in ascertaining the original constitution of the Church is indeed greater than he can easily conceive who has not attended to the power of prejudice. The controversies on the subject have been so acrimonious, and the tendency to confound Christianity with a mere system of what is called *Natural Religion,* is in the present age so very prevalent, that few men have brought to the enquiry minds so completely divested of prepossession, as to be capable of judging impartially. The truth may be detailed in the sacred Scriptures with sufficient clearness; but we all study the Scriptures under a bias, more or less powerful, in favour of the party to which we belong; and that bias, especially if we have ourselves been engaged in controversy, is very apt to prevent us from seeing what is written even as with a sun-beam. We may be ambitious of making *discoveries* in theology and of becoming the founders of new sects; and such ambition must necessarily impel us to differ as much as possible from the luminaries of antiquity, that we may display the vigour of our own minds, and our superiority to what we are pleased to call prejudice. Or we may be so attached to antiquity as to consider every prejudice and every rite of the primitive Church, as of perpetual obligation—not distinguishing between what was deemed essential, and what was even then considered as only expedient, in consequence of the circumstances in which the Church was placed."—*Mosheim's Ecclesiastical History*, Appendix I., vol. vi., p. 75. London, 1811. By the late Bishop Gleig.

That the apostolical succession should create much disturbance and opposition, among those denominations of Christians who have thrown off the primitive government of the Catholic Church, is not wonderful; but it does excite almost equally our wonder and our sorrow, that members, and even clergymen, of our own Church, should not only themselves be indifferent to this succession, but should censure, in no measured terms, those faithful champions who have boldly come forward, in the Church's hour of need, to defend this great bulwark of her visible existence.

An author familiarly known and much admired by many religious persons, in a pamphlet recently published, writes in the following terms:—

" It is painful to see that the spirit of boasting in apostolical succession, and peculiar regard to antiquity, in our own Church—for we, alas! began this unhallowed strain—has led our sister Church in Scotland, on the occasion of their late anniversary of the second centenary of their General Assembly, in 1838, when the foundations of the present system of their Church were laid, to a similar boastfulness, in their statements of the peculiar excellencies of their own constitution. The account of these proceedings at Glasgow, as given in the *Scottish Guardian* of December 21, 1838, must, I think, have pained humble and contrite Christians. Oh, we none of us do well to boast in our institutions and their excellencies: humiliation before God is our honour and our safety."—*Remarks on the Dangers of the Church of Christ.* By the Rev. Edw. Bickersteth, rector of Watton, Herts. London, 1839.

Now why, in this age of hostility against the Church, her pious and able defenders should be charged with the "spirit of boasting in apostolical succession," is not very easy to understand, especially when it comes from one within the camp—from an ordained clergyman of the Church.

Again, what Churchman—unless he merge the Church visible in the *in*visible, whereby he virtually ceases to be a Churchman—can designate the Presbyterian Establishment of Scotland "*our sister Church in Scotland?*" Our sister Establishment it may very properly be called, not "our sister Church." Nor, on the principles of an Episcopalian, and the bounden and binding principles of a clergyman of the Church of England, can the Church be properly spoken of as "*our* institution." The institution of the CHURCH was by Christ and His Apostles: it is therefore DIVINE. The *establishment* may be said to be *ours*; for it is of *human* institution.

But this has no reference to the "apostolical succession."

This divine institution admits not of "boasting," nor by its champions is it "boasted" of. It should be uncompromisingly held. The citadel should be defended; and the providence of God has raised up faithful soldiers, like those on the walls of Jerusalem, to rebuild and maintain her walls; boldly to defend the towers and bulwarks of our Zion, through the influencing power of the interior spirit of faith; and, in the noble language of no mean Christian warrior, to aid in that work which " the pious believer sees with the eye of faith—the miraculous support and preservation of the Church from the attacks of open enemies, the treachery of false friends, and the intemperate or lukewarm zeal of its weaker members."—*Bp. Horsley's Sermons on our Lord's Resurrection.* First edition, p. 167.

" Our humiliation before God" is surely no way touched or diminished by our determined resistance to the enemies of His Church. I fear rather that the weak abandonment of this our solemn ordination vow, and the more than infirm compliance with all other denominations of Christians in matters wherein they decidedly differ, and depart from the Church, because they may agree with ourselves in some peculiar doctrines or dogmas which we cherish, savour more of the "treachery of false friends," and more often cloak both intellectual and spiritual pride, than that they can possibly be characterized as "humiliation before God." That "humiliation," one of the most heavenly gems of the Christian coronet, is itself endangered by such compromise. Our honour and our safety are put in peril rather than secured.*

That our great Reformers used very different language on this great church principle of "apostolical succession" is matter of indubitable verity. It should, however, be more generally known. I therefore transcribe the following passages on this subject from a recent publication of a well-known sound divine:—

---

* See some judicious remarks of Archbishop Whately on the true sources of "Christian Humility," in his Essay on the "Dangers arising from injudicious Preaching." Sect. V., Essays, page 37. London, 1839.

"The words of Cranmer are—

"'The holy Apostle St. Paul, good children, in the tenth chapter of his Epistle to the Romans, writeth on this fashion—" Whosoever shall call upon the name of the Lord shall be saved. But how shall they call on Him on whom they believe not? How shall they believe on Him of whom they have not heard? How shall they hear without a preacher? How shall they preach except they be sent?" By the which words St. Paul doth evidently declare unto us two lessons.

"'The first is, that it is necessary to our salvation to have preachers and ministers of God's most holy word to instruct us in the true faith and knowledge of God.

"'The second is, that preachers must not run to this high honour before they be called thereto, but they must be ordained and appointed to this office, and sent to us by God. For it is not possible to be saved, or to please God, without faith; and no man can truly believe in God by his own wit (for of ourselves we know not what we should believe), but we must needs hear God's word taught us by others.

"'Again, the teachers, except they be called and

sent, cannot fruitfully teach. For the seed of God's word doth never bring forth fruit, unless the Lord of the harvest do give increase, and by His Holy Spirit do work with the sower. But God doth not work with the preacher whom He hath not sent; as St. Paul saith—" How shall they preach if they be not sent?" Wherefore it is requisite that preachers should be called and sent of God; and they must preach according to the authority and commission of God granted unto them, whereby they may strengthen men's belief, and assure their consciences that God hath commanded them to preach after this or that fashion. For else every man should still be in doubt, and think after this sort—" Who knoweth whether this be true which I hear the preacher say? Who can tell whether God hath commanded him to preach these things or no? And in case he teacheth nothing but truth, yet I am not sure that God will work with me as the preacher promiseth; perchance these promises pertain to other, and not to me." These doubts, in the time of temptation, might trouble men's minds, if we were not assured that our Lord Jesus Christ Himself hath both ordained and appointed ministers and preachers to teach His holy word and to minister His sacraments; and also hath appointed them what they shall teach in His name, and what they shall do unto us. Therefore he called them and sent them, and gave them instructions what they should do, and speak to us in His name, to the intent that we should give sure credence unto their words, and believe that God will work with us according to His words by them spoken. And He hath promised, therefore, that whatsoever they should bind upon earth should be bound in heaven; and whatsoever they should loose upon earth should be loosed in heaven. Wherefore, good children, to the intent you may steadfastly believe all things which God, by His ministers, doth teach and promise unto you, and so be saved by your faith, learn diligently, I pray you, by what words our Lord Jesus Christ gave this commission and commandment to His ministers, and rehearse them here word for word, that so you may print them in your memories, and write them the better when you come home. The words of Christ be these:—

"'OUR LORD JESUS CHRIST BREATHED ON HIS APOSTLES AND SAID, RECEIVE THE HOLY GHOST: WHOSE SINS YE FORGIVE, THEY ARE

FORGIVEN UNTO THEM: AND WHOSE SINS YE RESERVE, THEY ARE RESERVED.

"'Now, good children, you shall employ yourselves not only to rehearse these words without book, but also to understand what our Lord Jesus Christ meant by them; that when you shall be asked any question herein, you may make a direct answer, and that also in time to come you may be able to instruct your children in the same. For what greater shame can there be, either in the sight of God or man, than to profess thyself to be a Christian man, and yet be ignorant in what place of Scripture, and by what words, Christ commanded faith and forgiveness of sins to be preached—seeing that a Christian man ought to believe nothing as an article of his faith, except he be assured that either it is God's commandment or His word.

"'Now, good children, that you may the better understand these words of our Saviour Christ, you shall know that our Lord Jesus Christ, when He began to preach, He did call and choose His twelve Apostles; and afterwards, besides those twelve, He sent forth threescore and ten disciples, and gave them authority to preach the Gospel. And a little before His death and passion He made His prayer to His Heavenly Father for them, and for all those who should believe through their preaching, as it is declared in the Gospel of St. John. Now it is not to be doubted but that Christ's prayer was heard of His Heavenly Father; wherefore it followeth, that as many as believed the preaching of Christ's disciples, were as surely saved as if they had heard and believed Christ Himself. And after Christ's ascension the Apostles gave authority to other godly and holy men to minister God's word, and chiefly in those places where there were Christian men already, which lacked preachers, and the Apostles themselves could no longer abide with them; for the Apostles did walk abroad into divers parts of the world, and did study to plant the Gospel in many places. Wherefore, where they found godly men, and meet to preach God's word, they laid their hands upon them, and gave them the Holy Ghost, as they themselves received of Christ the same Holy Ghost, to execute this office.

"' And they that were so ordained were indeed, and also were called, the ministers of God, as the Apostles themselves were, as Paul saith unto Timothy. And so the ministration of God's word (which our Lord Jesus Christ Himself did first institute) was derived from the Apostles unto others after them, by imposition of hands, and giving the Holy Ghost, from the Apostles' time to our days. And this was the consecration, orders, and unction of the Apostles, whereby they, at the beginning, made bishops and priests, and this shall continue in the Church even to the world's end. And whatsoever rite or ceremony hath been added more than this, cometh of man's ordinance and policy, and is not commanded of God's word.

"'And on the other side, you shall take good heed, and beware of false and privy preachers, which privily creep into cities, and preach in corners, having none authority, nor being called to this office. For Christ is not present with such preachers, and therefore doth not the Holy Ghost work by their preaching, but their bud is without fruit or profit, and they do great hurt in commonwealths. For such as be not called of God, they, no doubt of it, do err, and sow abroad heresy and naughty doctrine. And yet you shall not think, good children, that preachers, which be lawfully called, have authority to do or teach whatsoever shall please them. But our Lord

Jesus Christ hath given them plain instructions what they ought to teach and do; and if they preach or do any other thing than is contained in their commission, then it is of no force, nor he ought not to regard it, nor ought we to regard it. And for this cause our Saviour Christ did breathe into His disciples, and gave them the Holy Ghost. For where the Holy Ghost is, there He so worketh that He causeth us to do those things which Christ hath commanded; and when that is not done, then the Holy Ghost is not there. Wherefore all things which we shall so speak or do can take none effect.'—*Cranmer's Sermon on the Apostolical Succession and Power of the Keys. Anglican Fathers*, pp. 19-23.

"To this we may add the following from Bishop Jewell:—

"'Therefore, the ancient Father Irenæus giveth us this good counsel: "Eis, qui sunt in ecclesiâ, presbyteris obaudire oportet, qui successionem habent ab Apostolis, qui, cum episcopatûs successione, charisma veritatis certum, secundum beneplacitum Patris, acceperunt." It becometh us to obey those priests in the Church which *have their succession from the Apostles*, and, together with the succession of their bishoprics, according to the good will of God the Father, have received the undoubted gift of the truth.'—*Defence of Apology*, part ii., chap. 5.

"Mr. Vogan, from whose able and argumentative visitation sermon I have taken this quotation, observes that, 'though Bishop Jewell, in his "Defence," sometimes appears to make little of the succession, this was only in comparison with right faith, and under the view of the succession being unaccompanied by right faith.'

"'One of the falsehoods propagated in these days is, that the Reformers did not hold the divine right of Episcopacy, but that this doctrine was subsequently introduced. That our Reformers were very generally of opinion that, where Episcopacy could not be had, ordination by presbyters might, as a *temporary* measure, be tolerated—just as grace will be given to those who desire to receive the sacraments, but from circumstances are unable to do so—is not to be denied; and I am not aware that any Churchmen of the present day would disagree with them in the opinion, although, among the Protestants abroad, there is not now the same excuse for their want of Episcopacy as there was in the time of the Reformation. But the *Episcopal suc-*

cession was assumed as a necessary doctrine of the Reformed Church of England on the very first public occasion, when our Reformers appeared in defence of the Reformation, after the accession of Elizabeth. At the authorized conference between the friends of the Reformation and the advocates of Romanism, to which allusion has before been made, Dean Horn, in the name of the Reformers, observes, " *The Apostles' authority is derived upon after ages, and conveyed to the bishops their successors."* Hence he contends for their Apostolical authority to reform their Churches without reference to the See of Rome, the bishop of that See being only the equal of other bishops. (*Collier*, ii., 418). The Puritans did not at first declare themselves hostile to Episcopacy, but as soon as they did so, the English Reformers asserted the authority of bishops as of divine right. Bishop Hutton maintained the doctrine, before Lord Burghley and Sir Francis Walsingham, with precisely the same arguments as those which are now employed. (*Strype's Life of Archbishop Whitgift*, iii., 224). Dr. Bancroft, too, defended the doctrine, that bishops were, *jure divino,* superior to the other clergy, even though the Puritans attempted to silence him by craftily bringing in political considerations, and by contending that it was inconsistent with the Queen's supremacy. (*Strype's Whitgift*, i. 559). In short, the divine right of Episcopacy was asserted before it was questioned, for men did not question at first what, for 1500 years, had been undisputed; and as soon as ever it was questioned, it was immediately defended, on scriptural grounds, by a bishop, and by the archbishop's chaplain.'"—*A Call to Union on the Principles of the English Reformation*: a Sermon preached at the Primary Visitation of Charles Thomas, Lord Bishop of Ripon. By Walter Farquhar Hook, D.D., &c.; with Notes and an Appendix, containing copious Extracts from the Reformers. London, 1839. p. 105.

NOTE B, PAGE 25.

WHO IS THE HERETIC?

"No man in religion is properly a *heretic* at this day, but he who maintains traditions or opinions not provable by Scripture, who, for aught I know, is *the Papist only—he the only heretic, who counts all heretics but himself."—Milton's Treatise of Civil Power in Ecclesiastical Causes. Prose works by Dr. Symmons,* vol. iii., p. 326.

In this able tract of our great poet there is much practical wisdom, tainted, however, with some Ultra-Protestantism. But the above sentence may be accounted the deliberate judgment of all Protestant Churches. It is, moreover, a just and an adroit mode of turning the tables upon the antagonist. But heretics of old were those who impugned the judgment of the Catholic Church, by the denial of cardinal doctrines of faith. Such was the *Arian heresy*, condemned by the great Council of Nice, at which the Emperor Constantine presided, of which the Nicene Creed is a monument.

NOTE C, PAGE 27.

PRINCIPLES OF THE CHURCH OF ENGLAND.

It is gratifying to find such works as that, of which the following fearless yet truly Christian and tolerant declaration of Church principles is an extract, published in the present day, when the Church is engaged in a struggle for her existence as an Establishment:—

"Whatsoever blessing God gives through His regularly ordained ministry; whatsoever benefit is attached to their ministration of the sacraments of baptism and the holy Eucharist; whatsoever advantage belongs to hearing the word preached by lawful sipritual authority—all these the Dissenter manifestly loses, whether it be through his sin or his misfortune. Thus, in a remarkable manner, the sin of the parents cleaves to the children until the third or fourth generation; for as I have heard remarked, and, as far as my own observation extends, believe it true, Dissenters, except of the more violent political sort, do, after a few generations, find their way back to the Church.

"So then we believe that the Church of Christ is one, and indivisible, and that God's providence will continually preserve it. Time, in its course, may for a while obscure the excellence of its beauty; it may be weighed down by heresy and error, as it was before the Reformation; but by the help of God, and through the light of His holy word, it will again emerge in its former purity. It may be vexed by schism, as it is at the present time; but with God's aid, it will shake off from it all its enemies and false friends, as it has done many times before. It will flow on like a mighty river, fertilizing the plains; though its current may run turbid for a while, or a thousand bubbles float upon its surface, yet will it go calmly and majestically onward till it falls into the ocean of eternity.

"(Herbert paused, but, his friend making no reply, he again resumed).

"The observations which I have made with regard to separation from the Church have been in answer to the latitudinarian opinions which are at present so lamentably prevalent. I am, however, very far from denying that there is also such a thing as intolerance and undue positiveness, as well as latitudinarianism. Each man, of course, endeavours to attain the true medium. In my opinion, the best way to avoid the two extremes is to make up one's mind as to what *is* the true Church of Christ, and, with thankfulness to God, to study to live in holy communion with it; not to care to pronounce decidedly who do *not* belong to it, or what disadvantage accrues to them. Church matters are so confused and involved, that it seems impossible to draw the precise line of demarcation between the Church and Separatists. With regard to the several bodies more immediately in contact with ourselves, which receive commonly the appellation of Churches, it does not seem necessary, or even possible, that we should affirm how far they have a right to that title, or rather, how far the individual members of those bodies may claim the title of Churchmen. We cannot admit their claim, because, in our judgment, they do not adhere to the Apostolic doctrine and discipline. On the other hand, to say precisely what degree of aberration excludes them from the rank of Churches would be doing more than we are warranted. Thus, the Church of Rome, miscalled the Catholic Church, while it maintains the Apostolic succession and threefold order of ministry, has, as we believe, especially at the Council of Trent, authorized gross errors, and departed in many things from the Apostolic doctrine, as set forth in holy Scripture. How far this may vitiate her ministrations, we presume not to judge. Hooker says, 'we must acknowledge even heretics themselves to be, though a maimed part, yet a part of the visible Church. We dare not communicate with Rome concerning her sundry gross and grievous abominations; yet, touching those main parts of Christian truth, wherein they constantly still persist, we gladly acknowledge them to be of the family of Jesus Christ.'

"So again with regard to Presbyterians—the doctrines which they hold are, in most respects, similar to our own, and they profess to maintain the Apostolic succession of the ministry;* but in rejecting the ordination of bishops, to whom alone, as we believe, power was given in the Church to ordain, they have introduced a perplexing novelty, and have departed from the Apostolic discipline, which had existed for fifteen hundred years. The power of ordination, which was conferred by the Apostles on the first bishops, has been handed down from bishop to bishop, throughout the whole Church, from the beginning; and we have no intimation, either

* See "An Apology for the Church of Scotland," by the Rev. J. Cumming, minister of the Scotch Church in London.

in Scripture or in history, of elders or presbyters having received the power to ordain, or to administer the sacraments, without Episcopal ordination. At the same time, I dare not assert, either, on the one hand, that their sacraments are unsanctified to those who piously receive them; or, on the other, that they are blessed in the same manner as when duly administered by those divinely commissioned for that purpose. These are points with regard to which it is by no means possible to pronounce decidedly. Though fully convinced that our own is the true Church, and that those who vary from it in essential points are so far in the wrong, we must leave to a higher authority to judge what consequences their error involves.

"As to the Dissenters, they do not believe at all in the doctrine of the one visible Church, and therefore, of course, do not profess to belong to it; they claim to be members, by faith, of the Church invisible. With regard to the salvation of individuals, we do not presume to speak. Until the judgment of the great day we cannot tell who will be members of Christ's invisible Church. 'The Lord knoweth whom He hath chosen;' we do not. 'Many shall come from the east and from the west, and shall sit down with Abraham, Isaac, and Jacob, in the kingdom of heaven; but the children of the kingdom shall be cast into outer darkness.' So, many Dissenters, many Romanists, and even Heathens, will, we may hope, eventually be saved; while many lukewarm, indolent, unfaithful Churchmen will be condemned. 'Let us, therefore, not be high-minded, but fear.'

"Still we believe, and rejoice in the belief, that we, who are baptized members of the one Catholic and Apostolic Church, have been called to high privileges and advantages; and that the inheritance of glory is actually sealed and made over to us. May God make us thankful, as we ought to be, and give us grace to use our privileges to His glory and our own salvation!"*— *Portrait of an English Churchman.* By the Rev. W. Gresley, M.A. London. 1839. pp. 57-62.

The conscientious Churchman, especi-

---

* "The true Church is the universal fellowship of God's faithful and elect people, built upon the foundation of the Apostles and Prophets, Jesus Christ being the head corner-stone. And it hath always three notes or marks whereby it is known—pure and sound doctrine, the sacraments ministered according to Christ's holy institution, and *the right use of ecclesiastical discipline.*"—*Homily for Whit-Sunday.*

ally the clergyman, is referred to the following cautionary passage of Dr. Mill, in an ordination sermon on "The Duties of an Apostolical Ministry."* After stating, with his accustomed ability, "the triple gradation of offices, of deacons, of priests, and of bishops"—and the "ancient foundation [of the Church]—the foundation, as we believe, of the Apostles and Prophets, Jesus Christ Himself being the chief corner-stone"—he thus affectingly warns the Churchman of his danger of resting in "EXTERNAL ORTHODOXY:"—

"But another train of reflection, my brethren, must be ours before we can make this subject one of congratulation or rejoicing to ourselves. There is scarcely any complacency less justified by sound reason than that which delights itself in an external orthodoxy, while the internal spirit is wanting, and which, in the ideal survey of sacred privileges conferred, overlooks alike their essential nature, and its own concern and

---

* Preached at St. John's Cathedral Church, Calcutta, at an ordination of deacons, on Palm-Sunday, April 4, 1830, and inscribed to Bishop Turner.

responsibility in them. It was this very error which caused the fall of the literal Israel, to whom belonged ' the adoption, and the glory, and the covenants, and the giving of the law, and the service of God, and the promises; nay, of whom, as concerning the flesh, Christ Himself came, who is God over all, blessed for ever.'*
The God, who, in just wrath at their senseless error, has signally fulfilled the sentence long before pronounced by their lawgiver, provoking them to jealousy by those which were no people, and raising up of the very stones to be children to Abraham, while he consigned those, the literal heirs of the promise, to the exterior darkness; will He be more tender to our far vainer and less founded self-complacency, if, forgetting all real obligation which the succession of an Apostolical ministry imports, we turn this to a subject of external distinction and fruitless glorying? May we not rather expect that He will shame us by those who have not the same advantage with ourselves?—that He will make the more visible piety and zeal of those who are without this succession, who even erroneously contemn

---

* Rom. ix. 3-25, xi. 11, *seq*., &c.; Cf. Deut. xxxiii.; Matt. iii. 9, viii. 11, 12, &c.; Apoc. ii. 5.

or deny its being, a means of awakening us to a salutary compunction—who would appear to pride ourselves in it, yet, in effect, slight and disregard it? Nay, may we not expect that our candlestick, like that of other Apostolical Churches before us, that have failed to give their light, may be removed from its place, and leave us not even the vain circumstance of its outward fabric to glory in? Such, indeed, if we consult the analogies of the divine proceeding elsewhere, is what we have too great reason to apprehend, unless we carefully review, in its true nature, the commission which has descended to us; a subject far from unimportant to any, but to those of us on whom the vows of God are already, or who are just about to undertake that irrevocable and indelible character, one of powerful and overwhelming interest."

Note D, Page 27.

"OF THE WORD 'PRIEST.'"

"The Greek and Latin words which we translate '*priest*' are derived from words which signify 'holy:' and so the word '*priest*,' according to the etymology, signifies him whose mere charge and function is about holy things, and therefore seems to be a most proper word to him who is set apart to the holy public service and worship of God, especially when he is in the actual ministration of holy things. Wherefore, in the rubrics, which direct him in his ministration of these holy public services, the word '*priest*' is most commonly used, both by this Church and all the primitive Churches, Greek and Latin, as far as I can find; and I believe it can scarce be found that in any of the old Greek or Latin Liturgies the word 'presbyter' was used in the rubrics that direct the order of service, but in the Greek, ἰερευς, and in the Latin, '*sacerdos*,' which we in English translate '*priest*,' which I suppose to be done upon this ground, that this word '*priest*' is the most proper for him that ministers, in the time of his ministration.

"If it be objected that, according to the usual acceptation of the word, it signifies him that offers up a sacrifice, and therefore cannot be allowed to a minister of the Gospel, who hath no sacrifice to offer; it is answered, that the ministers of the Gospel have sacrifices to offer (1 Pet. ii. 5). '*Ye are built up a spiritual house, a holy priesthood to offer up spiritual sacrifices*' of prayer, praises, thanksgivings, &c. In respect to these, the ministers of the Gospel may be safely, in a metaphorical sense, called *priests*, and in a more eminent manner than other Christians are, because they are taken from among men to offer up these sacrifices for others. But, besides these spiritual sacrifices mentioned, the ministers of the Gospel have another sacrifice to offer, *viz.*, the unbloody sacrifice, as it was anciently called—the commemorative sacrifice of the death of Christ, which does as really and truly show forth *the death of Christ* as those sacrifices under the law did foreshow it; and in respect of this sacrifice of the Eucharist, the ancients have usually called those that offer it up *priests*. And if *Melchizedek* was called a priest (as he is often by St. Paul to the Hebrews), who yet had no other offering or sacrifice, that we read of, but that of bread and wine, (Gen. xiv.) '*He brought forth bread and wine; and,* or, *for* (the Hebrew word bears both) *he was a priest*'—that is, this act of his was an act of priesthood; for so must it be referred, '*He brought forth bread and wine; for He was a priest;*' and not thus, '*and He was a priest, and blessed Abraham*' (for both in the Hebrew and Greek there is a full point after these words, *and*, or, *for He was a priest)*—if, I say, *Melchizedek* be frequently and truly called a *priest*, who had no other offering, that we read of, but *bread and wine*, why may not they whose office is to bless the people, as *Melchizedek* did, and, besides that, to offer that holy bread and wine, the body and blood of Christ, of which his bread and wine at the most was but a type, be as truly, and without offence, called *priests* also?

"If it be again objected, that the word *priest* is a Jewish name, and therefore not to be used by Christians, it is answered—

1. "First, that not everything that was Jewish is become unlawful for Christians to use. I find, indeed, that those things amongst the Jews that were shadows of things to come, are abolished now that Christ is come (Col. ii. 16, 17), and, therefore, to use them, as still necessary and obliging to performance, is unlawful under the Gospel, for it is virtually to deny Christ to be come (Gal. v. 3)—'*An entangling ourselves again in the yoke of bondage, from which Christ hath set us free.*' (Col. ii.) And, therefore, *St. Paul* tells the *Colossians* there, that he was *afraid of them*, for their superstitious observation of Sabbaths,

which were shadows of things to come: and in that chapter to the *Galatians* he does denounce damnation to them that *entangle themselves again in that yoke of bondage.* (v. 2). But that other things, rites, or usages of the Jews, which were no such shadows, should be unlawful to Christians, if they were used without such an opinion of necessity as we formerly spake of, I cannot persuade myself can ever be proved by either direct Scripture, or necessary inference from it. It will not, therefore, follow, that the name of *priest* (which is no shadow of things to come), though it were Jewish, would become unlawful to Christians.

2. " The names of those rites and ceremonies which were most Jewish, and are grown damnable to Christians, may still be lawfully used by Christians in a spiritual and refined sense. St. Paul, who tells us that the circumcision of the Jews is become so unlawful, that if it be used by Christians, with an opinion of the necessity aforesaid, it forfeits all their hopes of salvation by Christ (Col. ii. 2), uses the word circumcision frequently, particularly in that very chapter (ver. 11), '*In whom ye,* Christians, *are circumcised.*'

3. " The word *priest* is not a Jewish name—

that is, not peculiar to the Jewish ministry. For *Melchizedek*, who was not of *Aaron's* order or priesthood, is called a *priest* by St. Paul to the Hebrews often; and our Saviour is a *priest* after the order of *Melchizedek*: and the *ministers of the Gospel* are called *priests* by the Prophets (Isaiah xvi. 21; Jer. xxxiii. 17), where they prophecy of the times of the Gospel, as will appear by the context and ancient exposition.

"Lastly, St. Paul, where he defines a minister of the Gospel, as well as of the Law, calls him *priest*. (Heb. v. and viii.)

"To sum up all then. That name, which was not Jewish, but common to others; that name, which was frequently and constantly used by primitive Christians; that name, by which the Prophets foretell that the ministers of the Gospel shall be called; lastly, that name, by which St. Paul calls them, may not only lawfully, but safely, without any just ground of offence to sober men, be used still by Christians, as a fit name for the ministers of the Gospel: and so they may be still called, as they are by the Church of England in her rubric, *priests*."— *Bishop Sparrow's Rationale*, p. 339. Edit. 1684.

Note E, Page 28.

THE THREE ORDERS OF CHRISTIAN MINISTRY.

" That three orders of Christian ministry have subsisted ever since the calling of Aaron, and the divine institution of the Levitical priesthood, has ever been the opinion of all sound Churchmen, and must be the opinion of every one who is capable, by his learning and natural faculties, or is not incapacitated by indolence to examine, or by prejudice, to judge with tolerable impartiality. On the separation of the extraordinary gifts from the official character of the first preachers of the Gospel, and the analogy which subsists between the Jewish and Christian Church, the reader is referred to Archbishop Potter's unanswerable treatise of Church government. It has been justly remarked by Mr. Archdeacon Daubeny, in his 'Guide to the Church,' that the ' Jewish and Christian Church are to be considered not so much different establishments, as two editions, if we may so say, of the Church of God—the former constituting, as it were, the ground plan upon which the latter has been built.' Thus, when our Lord ministered, the Church consisted of three orders—Himself, as 'the Shepherd and Bishop of souls;' and under Him the twelve Apostles and seventy Disciples: forming a close analogy to the ministry under the law, which consisted of the high priest, the priests, and the Levites. After the death of our Lord, to keep up the three orders, we read that the Apostles ordained a *third* order, of deacons.

"The common objection against the first order, that the names of bishop and presbyter, which is unquestionable, are used the one for the other in the New Testament, is of no force; for this alters not the state of the question, as it is the *office*, not the *name*, for which we contend. All, however, who are at all acquainted with antiquity, know that the names of bishop and presbyter were at first the common names for all of the first and second order of the clergy: and at that time the appropriate name for bishops, to distinguish them from mere presbyters, was that of *Apostles*. These are the words of the ancient historian, Theodoret:—'The same persons were anciently called, promiscuously, both bishops and presbyters; while those, who are now called *Bishops*, were called *Apostles*. But in process of time, the name of Apostles was appropriated to such only as were Apostles indeed—namely, the twelve and St. Paul, and the name of bishop was restrained to those who before were called Apostles. Thus Epaphroditus was the Apostle of the Philippians, and Titus the Apostle of the Cretans, and Timothy the Apostle of the Asiatics.'*

"The texts referred to by Theodoret, when he wrote this, are decisive of the question. The Apostle to Timothy,† when he speaks of the office of a bishop, intends, perhaps, the office of a presbyter, because the qualifications of a deacon immediately follow. Whitby quotes three different opinions of the ancient Fathers—Theodoret, as above, Epiphanius, and Chrysostom, and others. The lowest opinion is, that 'the bishop is above the presbyter,' and that all ordinations which are not performed by the bishop are irregular, and performed by them who have no power to ordain.

"The Apostle to the Philippians writes, in the name of himself and Timothy, 'to all the saints in Jesus Christ which are at Philippi, with *the*

---

* Theodoret Com. in 1 Tim. iii. 1; in Phil. i. 1, ii. 25. See also Bingham's Eccl. Antiq., book ii., chap. 2; Mosheim's Eccl. Hist., vol. vi., p. 95.

† 1 Tim. iii. 1.

bishops and deacons'—συν επισκοποις και διακονοις.*
The best expositors† of this passage, both ancient and modern, are of opinion that St. Paul wrote to the presbyters and deacons of Philippi, because their bishop, Epaphroditus, whom he styles 'his brother, and companion in labour, and fellow-soldier, and *their Apostle,*'‡ was then with him at Rome. The words ὑμων αποστολον are very improperly rendered 'your messenger' in our translation; but the original language clearly points out the distinction between the *office* and the *name* of him who now exercises the office of an *Apostle* with the title of *Bishop;* out of respect, as Theodoret tells us, to those holy persons who 'were Apostles indeed.'"—*Note to an Ordination Sermon*, preached in the Episcopal Chapel at Stirling, October 18, 1826. By the Rev. B. Bailey, M.A., &c.

I may refer such readers as possess the publication to a masterly sermon on "the Duties of the Apostolical Ministry," by the learned Dr. Mill—from whom there is one extract in Note G—when Principal of

---

* Phil. i. 1.   † See Whitby in loc.   ‡ Phil. ii. 25.

Bishop's College, Calcutta, preached at an ordination held there on April 4, 1830; respecting whom see further the next note, F. The texture of the whole argument is so closely woven together, that it were scarcely possible to extract any isolated passage. Suffice it, that it fully bears out the arguments of the above note, and of the sermon to which that note was originally appended, and of the discourse to which this is an appendix.

NOTE F, PAGE 30.

THE CHURCH OF CHRIST.

"The Church (continues Bishop Gleig, who is the author of this very able dissertation), which Christ everywhere calls His kingdom, and which He declared to Pilate was not to be of this world, was founded by Himself, and built by His Apostles, acting under His authority; and its privileges, whatever they may be, are derived wholly from Him. No man could be admitted into the Church, or cast out of it, but by the authority which He conferred on the Apostles for these purposes; and, therefore, if the Apostles were to have no successors, the Church must have been swept from the face of the earth almost as soon as that ritual service which was established among the Jews, merely as preparatory to it. After the death of St. John, no man could either have been received into the Church, or cast out of it; and the Church itself must have perished with that generation. Yet Christ Himself solemnly promised, that 'against the Church,' to be built on the faith confessed by St. Peter, 'the gates of hell'—πυλαι ἀδου—the gates of *death*, or of the *receptacle* of the dead—'should never prevail;' for he well knew that the perpetuity of the Church is necessary to the perpetuity of the faith."

To the above extract may be appropriately added the following passage on the *Visible Church:*—

"We read, therefore, in this, as in other places of Scripture,* that while the Church of God is represented to us as a spiritual society, wholly

---

* Eph. iv. 4-16; 1 Cor. xii., &c.

spiritual in the principle and design of its incorporation, this is by no means intended to exclude the idea of its being a visible and organized one. There is a *body*, in the most perfect sense of the term, to which the unity of principle is as a living soul; and though, to pursue the image, the body without that unity of spiritual feeling were a mere machine, or rather a lifeless carcase, yet is this corporeal organization no less destined by the divine institution to be associated to that living principle, for the purpose of exhibiting and exemplifying the unity of saving doctrine to the world; nay, there are certain assigned and appropriate offices in the exterior community by which its spiritual existence is instrumentally maintained; and the very circulation of vital, healthful influence from the Omnipresent Head, through the several members of the body, is placed, as we have seen, as the result of that dispensation of the Holy Spirit that assigns their relative conditions to each, and apportions their several subordinated ministrations."—*Christian Unity:* a Sermon, preached at the Primary Visitation of the Right Rev. Daniel Lord Bishop of Calcutta, August 13th, 1834, by W. H. Mill, D.D., Principal of Bishop's College, &c.

Christian India has sustained an irreparable loss in the departure of Dr. Mill, as the head of Bishop's College, Calcutta, over which he ably presided as Principal for so many years. His attainments, as an oriental and a general scholar, are almost immeasurably great, as compared with scholars generally. But his greatest strength lies in his knowledge of the Scriptures, the fathers of the Church, and Christian antiquity. The loss of so gifted a man at a time like the present, when, in the Indian dioceses, as well as at home, SCHISM—described so finely by himself in this beautiful sermon on "Christian Unity," as " the painful *rent* (as the word *schism* implies) in that seamless garment which Christ made one"—is everywhere making way; when erroneous systems, so essentially dissentient as the so-called "Unity of the Church," by Mr. Baptist Noel, now industriously circulating by Dissenters in this colony, are put forth by a popular clergyman of the Church of England;* the loss, at such a season, " of such a noble champion of the Primitive and Apostolical Church, must, indeed, be felt throughout India, by every true Churchman, and by every admirer of Dr. Mill's great talents and vast attainments—all concentrated in the one great object of serving and illustrating the Catholic Church of Christ. His 'CHRISTA SANGITA, OR THE SACRED HISTORY OF OUR LORD JESUS CHRIST,' *in Sanscrit verse*," is one of the greatest achievements of oriental literature, by a scholar of the West, which is known in literary history. His English compositions are too few. Let us hope that they will be multiplied ere long, now that more literary leisure will be allowed him.† All

---

* The above was written in 1839-40, when Mr. Baptist Noel's pamphlet was circulated in Ceylon.

† This anticipation has been realized; for the writer of this note has received from the learned author copies of the first and second parts of Dr. Mill's able refutation of the " PANTHEISTIC PRINCIPLES" of the German school of Theology; and he

these faculties and attainments are possessed by a man as simple and natural in manners, and amiable in character, as he is gifted in intellect—a fact known to all who are privileged to be ranked among the friends of DR. MILL. May he long be spared to the Church he loves so entirely and serves so well, is the prayer of one friend now far distant from the beloved shores on which he treads!

"RARI QUIPPE BONI."

NOTE G, PAGE 32.

CALVIN, AND THE GENEVAN REFORMERS.

"Meanwhile, while the followers of Luther continued to acquire strength and numbers in Germany, they almost disappeared in France under the superior influence of a native Reformer. John Calvin was born at Noyon, in Picardy, in 1509, and imbibed or increased a

believes the work, as it is composed by the gifted *Christian Advocate* of Cambridge, will be published in parts.

strong attachment to Protestantism in the College of Forteret, at Paris. A speech, replete with Lutheran maxims, pronounced on one occasion by the rector of the College, was traced, at least in part, to the pen of Calvin, who, in order to escape a threatened arrest, fled to Angouléme. During his concealment in that town, he found sufficient access to books to compose the most elaborate and methodical work which had hitherto been written, illustrative of the Reformed principles—his '*Christianæ Religionis Institutio;*' that bold treatise appeared in print, for the first time, at Basle, in 1536, prefaced with a long, fearless, learned, and eloquent remonstrance to Francis I., whose hands were yet reeking with the blood of martyrs to Protestantism.*

"The early travels and various residences of Calvin are much disputed; and their adjustment matters but little in this place, since his histori-

---

* "The first edition known to bibliographers is that of Basle, 1536. The dedication bears date August 1, 1536, which has occasioned a suspicion, by no means well founded, that there *may be* an edition of that year also. The last copious revisions and augmentations by the author were given in a folio edition, at Geneva, 1559."

cal and ecclesiastical importance depends altogether upon his final settlement at Geneva. That city, long struggling against the encroachments of the Dukes of Savoy and of its own bishops, to whom the emperors had given a large share of temporal power, under the title of Princes of Geneva and its environs, was roused to new exertions for liberty at the epoch of the Reformation. Its inhabitants, uniting themselves in a solemn compact with those of Friburg and Basle, assumed the title of *Eictgenossen*, or sworn confederates; one of the conjectural sources of the better known party name *Huguenot*, applied afterwards to the Protestants of France. So powerful had the Genevese rendered themselves in the year 1526, that the Duke of Savoy abandoned his pretensions to sovereignty. Within nine years from that date the Reformed doctrine also had become so entirely naturalized among them, that it was proclaimed the religion of the State; the Popish bishop was excluded; and Calvin, by that time notorious for his zeal, his talents, and his intrepidity, received an invitation to fix his residence in the city, as a public teacher of religion. The earnest adjuration of William Farel (whom we have already seen at

Meaux, and who had been one of the most ardent promoters of the late revolution at Geneva) was not likely to be without effect upon a disposition so fitted to receive strong impressions as that of Calvin; and when he was solemnly warned, that unless he became a fellow-labourer in the vineyard of Geneva, the curse of God would attend him whithersoever he went, it was but natural that his kindled imagination should accept the fervid wish of his friend, as a special call from heaven. But the city was at that moment feverish and unsettled, in its first subsidence after a great religious and political change. Factious and fiery spirits were found in it not yet prepared to bow down to discipline; strong passions warred abroad unwilling to be controlled, and the stern and uncompromising temper of the new pastor was ill adapted to soothe them into repose and submission. Scarcely a year had passed from his first settlement before the inflexible severity with which Calvin pressed certain indifferent matters, as if they were essential, and the ill-judged pertinacity with which he sought to feed with strong meat, that infant Church which required the milk of babes for its sustenance, occasioned his forcible ejection. The points in controversy speak for themselves. In opposition to a decree of the Synod of Lausanne, he refused to allow the observance of any holidays excepting Sundays, to admit baptismal fonts to be placed within his churches, and to administer the sacrament with unleavened bread. Resistance to these harmless customs, wholly uninfluential as was their admission or rejection, upon purity, either of faith or practice, appeared to Calvin of sufficient moment to justify the sacrifice of his newly-embraced spiritual charge; and, in obedience to a decree of the Syndics, he retired in banishment to Strasburg.*

"During his absence men's thoughts and opinions grew calmer; the heat generated by sudden and rapid transitions had time to abate; and the want of a commanding and presiding mind,

* "Farel retired together with Calvin. We hear much of him afterwards from Meurisse. On one occasion, when a Cordelier was preaching on 'the perpetual virginity of the mother of God,' and that which the Bishop of Madanso, with a singular choice of epithets, terms *l'amoureuse incarnation* of our Saviour, Farel having interrupted the sermon, and denied the assertion, lost his hair and beard under the nails of the women present, who would have killed him, but for the seasonable appearance of a detachment of soldiers."—*Hist. de l' Hérésie dans Metz.* p. 67.

which might arrange, fashion, and consolidate the hitherto passing elements of their ecclesiastical polity, directed the wishes of the Genevese once again to Calvin. On his side it was not likely that difficulty should arise. A restoration sought for by his disciples ensured him unlimited dominion; the spiritual government of a distinguished and now independent city was in itself a most honourable charge; and the prospect of future success in the labour of holiness, of pouring the full light of the Reformation over France, immediately adjoining, and as yet but partially illuminated, might awaken in Calvin's bosom a glorious hope that he was set apart as the chosen Apostle of his native country. He accepted the proffered charge accordingly, 1541; and his brilliant visions were in great part realized. Never was more despotic sway established over men's wills and consciences than that which he erected in Geneva; and although he failed to introduce his scheme as the dominant religion of France, it became the real model, as himself was the virtual high priest of every separate Reformed congregation within the limits of that kingdom.

" His creed, which differs widely, in many respects, from some opinions frequently inculcated in his name, may be most accurately learned from the '*Christian Institution*' which we have already mentioned; and for his discipline, it is more our object to state what he *did*, than to enquire whether it was the best which might have been done.

"For the maintenance of his own personal authority no system assuredly could be better calculated than that which he arranged; nor would it be just on that account to condemn him as labouring chiefly for his own aggrandizement. That Calvin was influenced, in part, by ambition, it would be idle to deny; for what man has ever produced great effects upon his species if wholly devoid of that passion—a passion, when purified and defœcated, amongst the noblest engrafted on our nature? And Calvin's ambition *was* thus sublimed. The work which he took in hand was not his own work, but that of his Master; in order to perform it to the utmost, an extraordinary measure of power was necessary, and he therefore omitted no effort to obtain, no vigilance to preserve, his supremacy. That he did not mistrust his own use of that power can never be a matter of surprise; that he saw its danger if transmitted to others is evident from his not having recommended a successor, and from Beza's immediate advice after his friend's death* that the office of president should be allowed to expire with him. The infallibility, in all but name, which he maintained while alive, was too precious and too perilous a legacy to be bequeathed to a successor.

"The chief distinction of Calvin's ritual worship from that of Luther was found in its extreme plainness—a simplicity in too many instances degenerating into absolute nakedness. Not only were images and pictures excluded from his sacred edifices, as idols and abominations, but the decent majesty of devotion was violated by the rejection of almost every outward adjunct.

---

* "Spon, Hist. de Geneve, i., p. 313, note. Mosheim, iv. 375. Maclaine, in his note on Mosheim, has not only given wrong reference to Spon, but he has misrepresented facts. He states that Calvin, when at the point of death, advised the clergy not to elect a successor, and proved to them the dangerous consequences of intrusting any one man during life with authority so unlimited as that which himself had exercised. In the speeches reported in the notes to Spon, as delivered by Calvin on his death-bed, nothing of this kind occurs. But it is said that, when his infirmities prevented his regular attendance as president, Beza acted as his deputy; and that *he*, after Calvin's death, advised the substitution of an annual moderator, instead of a perpetual president."

The peculiar vestments which discriminated the priest from the layman were torn away; the soul-awakening tones of the organ were silenced; a frugal meal, eaten at a plain table, was substituted for the more ceremonious administration of the sacrament of the body and blood of the Saviour. It seemed as if Calvin believed that the senses were no longer the channels through which the mind received its knowledge and exhibited its operations; and that to omit paying the homage of the body was the genuine mode of worshipping God in spirit. The flight of her bishop prevented the continuance of Episcopacy in the Church of Geneva, although it by no means appears that Calvin himself was an enemy to that institution; and it would be difficult to establish a necessary connection between his polity, from which it was excluded by compulsion, and later voluntary Presbyterianism. The caprice of the congregation was allowed to regulate the salaries of the ministers, who were thus placed under the control of the very persons whom it was their duty to teach and to reprove, in season and out of season, through good report and evil report; and upon whom, if it were only on that account, they ought to be wholly independent. Besides the minister, each church appointed deacons, who acted as treasurers and almoners; and elders, who fulfilled the office of censors and guardians of public morals. Auricular confession indeed was abolished, but the inquisition of the consistory formed by the union of the above three authorities—the ministers, the deacons, and the elders—might prove equally dangerous, and was certainly far more tyrannical than the Romish custom. Once in every month this formidable band assembled; received the denunciations of the elders; summoned their erring brethren before their bar; took cognizance of their frailties; sentenced them to public penances; and enrolled their shame in everduring registers. A synod, composed of deputies from the several consistories, met annually to decide on matters of general interest; and in cases of extreme necessity an appeal lay to a council, to which representatives were furnished by all the provinces embracing Calvinism."*— *History of the Reformed Religion in France.* By the Rev. Edward Smedly, M.A., &c. Three vols. 12mo. London, 1832. Vol. i., pp. 35-38, 39-42.

* "The diffiulties under which Calvin laboured, and the wisdom which he manifested in encountering

For a full account of the French Huguenots the reader is referred to the above interesting work, which forms one of the many delightful and instructive publications of the theological library.—See also *Mosheim's Ecclesiastical History*, cent. xvi., c. ii., sect. 34, vol. iv., p. 87. London, 1811.

Note H, Page 33.

CREEDS OF THE CHURCH: AND THE EPISCOPAL CHURCHES OF SWEDEN AND NORWAY, AND OF DENMARK AND ICELAND.

Dr. Hook—who has since become so well known in the Church of England as one of her ablest and most uncompromising champions, in, I believe, his first, and perhaps his best sermon, made known to the public* many years ago—clearly lays down

them, are noticed at much length in the masterly preface to Hooker's 'Ecclesiastical Polity.'"

* "An Attempt to Demonstrate the Catholicism of the Church of England, and the other Branches of the Episcopal Church: in a Sermon preached in

the design and origin of CREEDS being composed, and used in the public services of the Church, with special reference to that of " the Catholic and Apostolical Church," in the Nicene Creed. One passage is too excellent not to be introduced from the text, to which he appends a note on the Lutheran Episcopal Churches of Denmark, Norway, and Sweden, which I shall likewise extract:—

"The design of a creed is *not* the expression of all that we believe, *but* the profession of certain truths, which, although denied by some, are maintained by *us*. There is, consequently, an antithesis to every article. We profess to believe in God the Father, *because* the Pagan rejects him; in God the Son, *because* the Arian blasphemes him; in God the Holy Ghost, *because* his personality is denied by the Macedonian. Now if, in the profession of belief in the existence

the Episcopal Chapel at Stirling, on Sunday, March 20, 1825, at the Consecration of the Right Rev. Matthew Henry Luscombe, L L. D." This very able sermon was inscribed to the Scotch bishops, and published by Rivingtons, London, 1825. 4to.

of the Catholic Church, the primitive Christians had intended nothing further than the acknowledgment of the existence of large masses of believers in the name of Christ, scattered over the face of the earth, no one in his senses would have objected to that which was self-evident. To have denied it would have involved an absurdity too gross for the most weak and illiterate of mankind to have been guilty of; and to have inserted the article in the Creed would, in consequence, have been at least a work of supererogation. But if, on the other hand, they intended, as we maintain, to distinguish by that title the true and Apostolic Church from the different sects of schismatics and heretics, *then* they asserted a fact against which those sects would originally contend, and *then*, also, we can readily account for its adoption in the various symbols or creeds of the Church."

He then goes on to state that this article was first added to the creed of Nice by the Council of Constantinople, in the year 381, according to the seventh canon of that Council; making a manifest distinction between the various schismatics and heretics, and "the Catholic and Apostolic Church of God."

"And let it be particularly observed, that among the schismatics specified in the seventh canon, and alluded to as *without the pale of the Catholic Church*, are the Novatians—Novatians who differed less from the Church *then* than any one sect, whether Calvinistic or Lutheran, differs from it *now*—who were in faith Homoousians, and in doctrine Episcopalians. Their only distinguishing characteristic was the uncompromising rigour of their discipline; so that if the Novatians were not considered as members of the *Catholic* Church, to that high privilege no other sect surely could prefer a claim." (pp. 16, 17).

To this last passage the following note is referred :—

"The Lutherans of Denmark, Norway, and Sweden, being Episcopalians, are of course exceptions to the assertions made in the text. The want of a detailed account, both of the doctrine and history of these Churches, is much to be regretted. An opinion is certainly entertained by some persons, to the prejudice of the Danish Episcopacy, that the German superintendents having sometimes assisted at the consecration of their bishops, the line of succession has been vitiated. It is desirable, therefore, that this subject should be placed in its proper light, in order that it may appear how far it would be conducive to the great end of unity for the other branches of the Reformed Catholic Church to enter into correspondence, and, upon their renunciation of their peculiar doctrine of consubstantiation, into communion with them."

In the text, when the sermon (to which this is the appendix) was delivered—in the haste of such compositions mechanically, however carefully they may be endeavoured to be thought out—I mentioned the Church of Sweden alone, as standing for the whole. But, whether or not their Episcopacy be equally pure, the Churches of Denmark and Norway have generally been esteemed to be connected with Sweden; and always, however the political and national positions of the countries may have changed, of the same doctrine and discipline as Lutheran Episcopal Churches, and, I believe, in communion with each other. We are prevented from communion with any of these Lutheran Churches by their peculiar doctrine of consubstantiation. In all other respects—of faith, doctrine, discipline, and Church government—I believe they resemble our Reformed branch of the Catholic Church. Of the pure Episcopacy of Sweden there is no doubt.

I have made some enquiry into the external history of these Churches, with the aid of such books as lie within my reach; but of their doctrine I have discovered nothing new or decided. It should be mentioned that Iceland, of which I shall give full details hereafter, is also an Episcopal Church of the Lutherans and a dependency of Denmark. In 1538 the Reformation was firmly established in Denmark under Christian III.; and the following year "it extended even to the frozen shores of Iceland."—See *Milner's History of the Church*, cent. 16.

"The Reformed religion was propagated in *Sweden* soon after Luther's rupture with *Rome*, by one of his disciples, whose name was Olaus Petri, and who was the first herald of religious liberty in that kingdom. The zealous efforts of this missionary were powerfully seconded by that valiant and public-spirited prince, Gustavus Vasa Ericson, whom the Swedes had raised to the throne, in the place of Christiern, King of Denmark, whose horrid barbarities lost him the sceptre that he had perfidiously usurped."—*Mosheim's Eccl. Hist.*, vol. iv., pp. 78, 79.

The Papal empire in Sweden was finally overthrown by this wise prince; and the king was the head of the Church, as in England. The revenue of most of the bishops was superior to that of the sovereign himself. They possessed castles and fortresses that rendered them independent of the crown. Their power was dangerous to the State. They lived in the most dissolute luxury. The discipline of the Church was reformed, and the opulence and authority of the bishoprics was reduced within proper bounds. But the Church was provided with able pastors, and Episcopacy was and is the established religion of Sweden; but the influence of the clergy evidently is not upheld in that respectable, yet moderate, elevation in which it was, and still is, in England. Long may that influence be continued!

In Denmark the Reformation was received so early as 1525, and by the ardent desire of Christiern II. (who had been deprived of the throne of Sweden for his cruelty) to have his subjects instructed in the principles and doctrines of Luther. The Reformation was completed by Christiern III., a prince distinguished equally for his prudence and virtue. Episcopacy was retained as in Sweden, and on much the same scale. The translator of Mosheim denies that the Christian prudence of Christiern III. was so great as Mosheim represents it; for the equipoise of government was hurt by a total suppression of the political power of the bishops. In the room of bishops, Dr. Maclaine says that "Christiern created an order of men with the denomination of 'superintendents,'" who performed the spiritual part of the Episcopal office without the least shadow of temporal authority.*

This transaction seems to be inaccurately stated. The Danish Episcopacy was not of the king's creation, but derived, like all other Episcopacy, from the bishops; and whether they were called bishops or superintendents is of no importance.† The

---

* See Mosheim's Eccl. Hist., vol. iv., pp. 81-86.

† Since the above was written, I have met with the following passage in the preface of Dr. Hook (whose doubt as to the Danish Episcopacy I have already quoted from a prior publication) to "The Early Life and Professional Years of Bishop Hobart" —"It has of late years been ascertained, that while the Episcopal succession has certainly been preserved in the Church of Sweden it has been lost in the Church of Denmark, where the Episcopacy is only nominal." The more primitive usages still kept up in the Church of Sweden tend to confirm this asser-

king deprived them of *temporal* power; for Mosheim writes thus expressly of the Episcopacy of Sweden and Denmark:—

"It is, however, to be observed, that in the history of the reformation of *Sweden and Denmark* we must carefully distinguish between the reformation of *religious opinions*, and that of the *Episcopal order*. For these two things may appear to be clearly connected, yet, in reality, they were so distinct, that either of the two might have been completely transacted without the other. A reform of doctrine might have been effected, without diminishing the authority of the bishops, or suppressing their order; and, on

tion, of the accuracy of which, coming from so high an authority, we can have no doubt. Whether Norway has preserved or lost her Episcopacy, and whether Iceland derived her Episcopacy originally from Norway or Denmark, are questions yet, I apprehend, unsolved. There seems to be something so primitive in Iceland, that one is unwilling to believe that its Episcopacy can be but nominal. (See the details of that interesting people hereafter). The Church of England stands higher and more defined, as a pure branch of the Catholic Church, the more she is examined. She has all the marks of the *Consensus Veterum* required by Vincentius:—" In ipsâ item Catholicâ Ecclesiâ magnopere curandum est, ut id teneamus, *quod ubique, quod semper, quod ab omnibus* creditum est."

the other hand, the opulence and power of the bishops might have been reduced within proper bounds without introducing any change into the system of doctrine that had been so long established and that was generally received."*

The reformation of the clergy, however, was conducted, it would appear, both in Sweden and Denmark, with considerable violence. It was, as regarded the privileges and possessions of the bishops, rather a matter of political expediency than of religious obligation. Luther expostulated with Christiern III., and exhorted him to use his clergy with more lenity. The equipoise of the State, as already observed, was thus destroyed: nor does it appear that in any of these countries the due weight of the clergy in public affairs has ever been restored.

The Reformation appears to have made similar progress, and about the same time, in Norway, so intimately connected as that

* Mosheim's Eccl. Hist., vol. iv., p. 85.

country was with Denmark by the union of the two kingdoms. "The inhabitants of Norway (says a modern writer) now speak the same language that is used in Denmark, though their original tongue is the dialect now spoken in Iceland. They profess the Lutheran religion, under an archbishop established at Drontheim, with four suffragans—namely, Bergen, Staffanger, Hanmer, and Christiana."* Another writer, in the same voluminous work, thus speaks of the religion of the three countries:—

"The Lutheran doctrine is universally embraced through all Denmark, Sweden, and Norway; so that there is not another sect in these kingdoms. Denmark is divided into six dioceses —one in Zealand, one in Fenén, and four in Jutland; but the bishops are, properly speaking, no other than superintendents, or *primi inter pares*.†

* Encyclop. Britt., 3rd Edit., Article *Norway*.

† This seems a very questionable position, arising, it should seem, from the writer's confounding the civil power of a bishop in England with the spiritual power of a bishop everywhere.

They have no cathedrals, ecclesiastical courts, or temporalities. Their business is to inspect the doctrine and morals of the inferior clergy. The revenue of the bishops of Copenhagen amounts to about 2,000 rix-dollars, and this is the richest benefice in the kingdom. The clergy are wholly dependent on the government. They never intermeddle, nor are employed or consulted, in civil affairs. They, nevertheless, have acquired great influence, and erected a sort of spiritual tyranny over the minds of the common people, by whom they are much revered. They are, generally speaking, men of exemplary lives, and some erudition."*

Everything in the above account is satisfactory and consistent, except what the writer calls " a sort of SPIRITUAL TYRANNY erected over the minds of the common people" by the clergy; which, indeed, is contradicted by their exemplary lives, and the reverence in which they are held by the people. Another writer, therefore, in the same work,† in the History of Sweden,

* Encycl. Britt., 3rd Edit., Article *Denmark*.
† Encycl. Britt., 3rd Edit., Article *Sweden*.

gives a much more consistent account of the clergy; and they so much resemble each other as to be, in religion, almost the same people.

"Their religion, it is stated, is Lutheran, which was propagated by Gustavus Vasa, about the year 1523. The Archbishop of Upsal has a revenue of about 400*l.* a year, and has under him thirteen suffragans, besides superintendents, with moderate stipends. No clergyman has the least direction in the affairs of state; but their morals, and the sanctity of their lives, endear them so much to the people, that the government would repent making them its enemies. Their churches are neat, and often ornamented. A body of ecclesiastical laws and canons direct their religious economy."

During the 18th century the Lutherans of Sweden and Denmark continued to predominate, and the Established Church was under their government. In Sweden clerical representatives composed a part of the states or national council; but in Denmark the clergy had no share of political power. It is affirmed, moreover, that the superintendents, who, it is said, acted in lieu of bishops, were required by the rulers of the State to propagate the doctrine of passive obedience.* The frequent mention of Danish superintendents does seem to throw some shades of doubt upon the Danish Episcopacy, whether corrupted by the German superintendents assisting at the consecration, or by any other irregularity. Yet the NAME of superintendent, equivalent to bishop or OVERSEER, is in no way decisive of the question.† I know not that any work has appeared of late years to clear up this question of doubt.

Modern travellers, as far as I have met with them, do not throw much light on the present state of the Churches of Sweden, Denmark, and Norway. Lapland is at-

---

* Mosheim's Ecclesiastical History. vol. vi., p. 279. Continuation by Dr. Coote. See also p. 236 of the same volume.

† See Note E.

tached to the Danish Church, and has a bishop. Finland, which formerly belonged to the Swedish dominion, is still of the communion of the Swedish Church. Both Acerbi, an Italian traveller, who visited these countries in the years 1798 and 1799, and Dr. Clarke, the well-known English traveller, who went the same route in the year 1799, speak of the Church and the clergy, even in the remote parts of Lapland and Finland, generally, with respect. They were entertained at the houses of clergymen in those countries, and found them both enlightened and religious men. In conduct and in learning they were what clergymen ought to be.* A singular instance of the physical hardihood of the people of Lapland is adduced by Acerbi, which, at the same time, shows the observance of the rites of the Church in that re-

* Acerbi's Travels, in 2 vols. 4to., London, 1802, vol. ii., p. 123, and elsewhere. See also Dr. Clarke's Travels in Scandinavia, vol. i., p. 368, 4to. edition. London, 1819.

mote r gion. This is related of "a woman who crossed the mountains of ice and snow in the month of December, five days after her delivery of a child, in order to attend the prayers of what is commonly called Churching."*

With the avowed deficiency of information as to the precise situation and history of those interesting Reformed Churches,† we much regret that so sagacious a traveller as Dr. Clarke had not as strong a stimulus in his constitution or his pursuits to search out religious history, as he exhibited in science and antiquities. One passage, however, respecting Norway, amid our scarcity of information, is acceptable:

"Of the state of religion in *Norway* we had not an opportunity of making many observations. The morals of the people, especially of the lower

---

* Acerbi's Travels, vol. ii., p. 153.
† Bishop Heber, when a very young man, travelled in Norway and Sweden, but he gives no information as to the state of these Churches. Had his journey been in his later life, his attention would have been directed to them.

orders, are good; and, thus judging of the tree by its fruits, we saw no reason for complaint. Formerly there were many different sects in the country; and among these some like our Methodists: but at present all are united. There is nothing, therefore, of that sourness which is caused by Dissent; and which, as it tends to separate the members of society from each other, tends also to sap the very foundations of Christianity; thereby proving an observation of Montesquieu,* 'that the most true and holy doctrines may be attended with the very worst consequences, when they are not connected with the principles of society.'† He ends this very excellent paragraph with a remark, by no means so unexceptionable, as to the state of the Norwegians—'Perhaps we ought to assign as a reason for the religious unanimity in *Norway*, that the same degree of ardour in religious matters which is found in our own country, and which in *Great Britain* has of itself given birth to the schisms that divide the members of its Christian community, has not yet been excited here. A great

* Esprit des Lois, liv. xxiv., c. 19, p. 161.
† Clarke's Travels in Scandinavia, vol. ii., p. 78, 4to. edit.

deal of what may be called *indifferentism* prevails on religious subjects among the *Norwegians*.'"

The religious differences in GREAT BRITAIN, it should be remembered, spring quite as much—and perhaps more—from POLITICAL differences, and political causes, and a partial or total indifference to religion, as from an excess " of ardour in religious matters." At all events, if those Norwegians have the " indifferentism" alleged by the traveller—and this is deeply to be deplored—they have not " the zeal without knowledge" of too many of our religious polemics, both within and without the Church; and when a more fervent spirit is kindled among them, let us trust that they will not have the many stumbling-blocks in the way of truth which obstruct her free course in Great Britain.

Since writing the above, I have met with the travels of William Rae Wilson, Esq., in Sweden, Norway, and Denmark, in the year 1824, which, though the author is a layman, and a Presbyterian, throw some light on the present state of those Churches, particularly of Sweden and Norway.

Of the worship at the cathedral at Gothenburg this traveller thus writes:—" In the cathedral, worship is performed three times on Sundays, according to the Swedish ritual. 'Prayers are read daily, and the sacrament regularly administered every Saturday and Sunday.'" (p. 25).

The preservation of a ritual is in strict conformity with our own Church. The frequency of communion is the preservation of the primitive usage, which we should do well to imitate and restore. "It was (says the author of the 'Ecclesiastical Antiquities') the rule and practice for all in general, both clergy and laity, to receive the communion every Lord's-day, except such as were unqualified for it, either as catechumens or penitents."* The canons

* Bingham's Eccl. Antiq., b. xv., chap. i., sect. 1. In this book it is shown, that on the Lord's-day, and

of the ancient Church, for the first three or four centuries, show, that as often as they met together for divine service on the Lord's-day, they were obliged to receive the Eucharist, on pain of excommunication.*

Compare this primitive piety of this Reformed Episcopal Church with the practice of the Reformed Presbyterian Establishment of Scotland. There (according to the rule of their Church) the sacrament of the Lord's Supper is administered not more, I think, than twice a year. In England, I grieve to say, our Church has sadly declined from this primitive and salutary usage of frequent communion at the Lord's table: whence pure religion has declined, and schism, and licentiousness of opinion and of manners, have supplied its place.

At the cathedral of Christiana, in Nor-

in many churches on other days, the Eucharist was always celebrated for at least the three first centuries.

* Bingham's Eccl. Antiq., b. xv., chap. i., sect. 1.

way (now united with the kingdom of Sweden*), Mr. Wilson describes the public service which he attended. On this occasion the sacrament was dispensed after the sermon. He remarks, however, that the same degree of seriousness and devotion was not observable by the Norwegians, as by the Swedes. (pp. 123, 124).

Again, at Carlstadt, in Sweden, where is "a Protestant church, built in the form of a cross, with a steeple and cross at the summit, the service was conducted with becoming solemnity." " When the clergyman pronounces the name of our Saviour, the hearers bow in token of reverence of this great Mediator." (pp. 153, 154).

This beautiful primitive act of reverence " at the name of Jesus" (Phil. ii. 10) is preserved in our own Church; and every pious Churchman must be gratified to see it kept up in a similar Episcopal Church,

---

* The treaty by which Norway was irrevocably renounced by Denmark, and annexed to Sweden, bears date 14th January, 1814.

such as Sweden. We have an express canon to this effect:* and yet there are now among us persons, and even clergymen, who, in their ultra-Protestant zeal, refuse to bow their heads at the name of the Redeemer. Such persons act in defiance of the canon of their own Church, and are rebuked by the primitive and reverential observance in the Reformed Church of Sweden.

The beginning of the Lord's-day at six o'clock on Saturday evening is also marked in the Swedish Church—at which our traveller is surprised, while he comments with just severity on revelry in the evening of the Lord's-day. But this is the

---

* The eighteenth canon—" When, in time of divine service, the LORD JESUS shall be mentioned, due and lowly reverence shall be done by all persons present, *as it hath been accustomed;* testifying by these outward ceremonies and gestures, their inward humility, Christian resolution, and due acknowledgment that the Lord Jesus Christ, the true eternal Son of God, is the only Saviour of the world, in whom alone all the mercies, graces, and promises of God to mankind, for this life, and the life to come, are fully and wholly comprised."

division of the day in our own Church, of which any one may satisfy himself by turning to the first rubric before the collect of Advent Sunday, which directs " that the collect appointed for every Sunday, or for any holiday that hath a vigil or eve, ' shall be said at the evening service next before.' " The custom of the Church now is, contrary to her ritual, to make the calculation from the termination of Saturday night to that of Sunday night; and I would not act contrary to this custom. But when pious Christians have for so many ages divided the day differently—when we see it so divided in foreign countries, and our own Prayer Book bears witness to it—we should not be so very intolerant of harmless associations, on Sunday evening, of families and intimate friends, not for revelry, but rational and religious conversation, sacred music, and other innocent and salutary enjoyments.

In almost all the towns he visited throughout Sweden the same decency of worship is attested by this really candid traveller. At Stockholm, in the principal church, the service is almost the same as that of the English Church. After the congregation have sung a Psalm, accompanied by the organ, prayers are read by the clergyman before the altar, when a second Psalm is sung. The clergyman mounts the pulpit and READS A SERMON, and this being finished, the clockerer, or clerk, receives the book from him, when the service concludes by repeating the singing. " A form of prayer is used here, as in the Church of England." (p. 227).

The notices of the church, and service, and clergy of Denmark, in Mr. Wilson's book, are less full, and in all respects less satisfactory. It almost induces the fear that some interference of the German superintendents, as hinted by Dr. Hook, may have disturbed the primitive purity and simplicity of the Danish WORSHIP, if not the succession of their Episcopacy. He gives the following account of the external government of the Church:—

"With regard to the supreme ecclesiastics of Denmark, there are nine dignitaries, who rank as bishops—one for Fionia, one for Lapland, four for Jutland, one for Sleswick, one for Holstein, and one for Iceland. At the period when Norway was under the Danish Government, four bishops were appointed for that country. Immediately after the Reformation in 1535, the high ecclesiastics were denominated superintendents, from the idea that the title of bishops savoured of [Roman] Catholicism. There is no archbishop, although there was one previous to the Reformation." (p. 455).

Whether or not the ordinations of the Danish Church have been interfered with by the German superintendents, who, though Lutherans, are Presbyterians, be an established or a questionable fact,* yet that their worship and services have de-

* On this subject see a note from Dr. Hook's Preface to the " Early Life, &c., of Bishop Hobart," ante p. 24.

clined from primitive purity, is too evident from the details of this intelligent traveller. He describes (p. 407) A CONFIRMATION, by an officiating minister, not a bishop; and the service " in the Royal Chapel at Copenhagen appeared to him to resemble the Presbyterian form of worship in Scotland." (p. 471).

One consolatory reflection, however, remains—that in Sweden, and Norway, and Denmark, the MORALS of the people are generally decent and good, their RELIGION uninfected with heresy, and their CHURCH undistracted by SCHISM.

Of ICELAND, a dependency of Denmark, we have more facts detailed than of the mother-countries and churches of northern Episcopacy. The physical phenomena of this wonderful island have attracted many of our scientific and intelligent countrymen to its shores. In this land of ice and perpetual snows on the elevated parts and summits of the mountains, the work of subterranean fire, in earthquakes, volcanoes, and hot springs of water, is exhibited to a degree unknown, perhaps, in any other part of the habitable globe. The people are in extreme poverty, yet attached most powerfully to their native soil: as one traveller, Sir George Mackenzie, appropriately cites of it—

" The shuddering tenant of the frigid zone
  Boldly proclaims that happiest spot his own."

In these dreary and inclement regions the Reformed Episcopal or Catholic Church is firmly established. Education is more solidly cultivated and more generally diffused than in happier climes; insomuch that the poorest labourer is commonly familiar with the Latin tongue. The people are simple and peaceable, and without vice. Religion is reverenced; and the ministers of the Established Church, though poor, are respected and beloved. Their poverty is indeed painful to be told; but their resignation and contentment are above all price.

APPENDIX.

Among the most interesting publications respecting this island and its inhabitants are the travels of Sir G. Steuart Mackenzie, who visited Iceland in the summer of 1810;* and "A Visit to Iceland in the Summer of 1834, by John Barrow, Jun."† From these works I shall make a few extracts on the Church and the clergy, and the state of religion generally. Sir George Mackenzie gives the following general outline:—

"The Reformation of Iceland took place A.D. 1551,‡ since which period the doctrine of the Lutheran Church, as it exists in the northern kingdoms of Europe, has been strictly maintained in the island. At the present time not a single dissentient is to be found from the established religion of the country; and the only instance of the kind on record is one which

---

* Travels in the Island of Iceland during the Summer of the year 1810. By Sir George Steuart Mackenzie, Baronet," &c. London, 4to., 1812.

† London, 12mo., 1835.

‡ Milner (see ante) says 1539. It was introduced at this earlier date, but probably not settled and established until 1551, as stated above.

occurred about the end of the second century, when Helgo Eiolfidas, a man who had acquired much knowledge of German literature, espoused the Socinian doctrines, and taught them openly to his children and friends, till compelled by the judgment of the Ecclesiastical Court to make a public renunciation of his belief. Doctrinal discussion is of course little known among the Icelanders; and the contests which have existed in their Church relate chiefly to external ordinances, and to the situation and rights of the clergy of the island.

" The religious establishment of Iceland is formed on a more extensive scale than might have been expected from the nature of the country and the condition of the people. The inhabited parts of the island are divided into one hundred and eighty-four parishes—a division which gives to each parish an average population of about two hundred and sixty persons. From the great extent, however, of these districts, it has in many instances been found necessary to erect more than one church in a parish; and the total number of churches in the island somewhat exceeds three hundred. The duty of each parish devolves upon a single priest, with the permission, however, if his own circumstances do not allow the full discharge of his duties, to take an assistant from among the young men educated for the Church, who have not yet obtained a permanent situation in life. The number of officiating ministers of religion is, of course, various at different times, though never greatly exceeding the number of the parishes. Immediately superior to the common priests are the provosts or deacons,* whose office it is to exercise a general superintendence over the churches in each syssel, and who are chosen in general from a regard to their talents and respectability of their characters. There are nineteen of these deacons in the island; but their number is included among that of the priests, just mentioned, as they severally have parishes attached to them, of which they discharge all the ordinary duties. A small additional stipend is attached to the office, which renders their situations somewhat superior to that of the other clergy."

Iceland was, during seven centuries, divided into two bishoprics. Since 1797 there has been but one.

* Probably the same as *archdeacon*.

"The bishop superintends the general concerns of the religious establishment. He inspects the conduct of the priests, regulates any ecclesiastical disputes which may occur, ordains those who are entering upon the pastoral office, and watches over the education and moral conduct of the people. It is a part of his duty also to visit, at stated periods, the different districts of his diocese, for the purpose of personal inspection; and the farmers of the country are required to assist him, while making these journeys, with every accommodation which their means may afford. The appointment of the bishop is vested in the Crown."*

"According to the official statement † procured by Dr. Hooker, the Bishop of Iceland draws about 1,800 dollars, or 360*l*., from the (Bessestad‡) school funds; the lecturer on theology, 600 dollars, or 120*l*. a year; and the inspector or steward (of the school), about 220 dollars, or 44*l*. a year, and receives for each of the scholars 60 dollars a year, or 4,000*l*. in the

---

* Sir G. S. Mackenzie, ut supra, p. 301.
† Barrow's Visit, p. 230.
‡ For the education of young men destined for the Church.

whole for their subsistence, and the two assistants 300 dollars, or 60*l.* a year each."

" The clergy are, for the most part, native Icelanders, and a great portion is taken from the students who have had their dimissus from Bessestad; but some few who can afford it send their sons to study at the University at Copenhagen. The number of parochial charges or livings is said to amount to somewhere about one hundred and ninety-four; but the number of the clergy is greater, as many of the parishes have two churches—the great distance, and the danger of travelling, particularly in the winter months, when the rugged fields of lava are covered with snow, making it impossible that the distant peasantry could attend at one church. The number of churches, therefore, together with what we should call chapels of ease, are stated to amount to about three hundred, to each of which is a clergyman; those who are beyond the number of the parishes, acting as assistants to the regular incumbents. From the great age of many of the incumbents, it is probable that not less than four per cent., or twelve, may die off annually.* Now, if we allow five years, on

* A moderate allowance; in the year 1834 the

an average, to each student at Bessestad, to complete his education, so as to qualify for holy orders, eight only will go off annually, and, therefore, one-third must be supplied from other sources. These sources are abundant; many of the clergy educate their sons at home, and also many of the peasantry, in the distant parts of Iceland more particularly. The education of the latter is superintended, in a very considerable degree, by the neighbouring clergymen. By the almost universality of this system of domestic education, there is not probably, in any part of the world, an agricultural, or rather pastoral, peasantry so well informed and enlightened as those of Iceland.

"We have it on the authority of former travellers in this country, and it is confirmed by the resident Danish merchants of Iceland, that it is no uncommon thing to meet with men labouring in the fields, mowing hay, digging turf, building the walls of their cottages, sheds, or cow-houses, and performing every kind of menial labour, who will write Latin, not merely with grammatical accuracy, but even with elegance.

number of British admirals that died was sixteen, being about ten per cent. of the whole.

"The season of out-door labour is so short, and the winter nights so long, that they have ample time afforded them to keep up and improve what they have learnt in their youth; they do not feel that manual labour is any degradation. Dr. Holland has well expressed this —'The summer's sun saw them, indeed, laboriously occupied in seeking their provision from the stormy ocean and a barren soil; but the long seclusion of the winter gave them the leisure, as well as the desire, to cultivate talents which were at once so fruitful in occupation and delight. During the darkness of their year, and beneath the rude covering of wood and turf, they recited to the assembled families the deeds and descent of their forefathers, from whom they had received that inheritance of liberty which they now dwelt among deserts to preserve.'

"The clergy almost naturally submit to every species of drudgery from necessity; their incomes are too small to allow them to hire and feed labourers; and nothing is more common than to find the parish priest in a coarse woollen jacket and trousers, or skin boots, digging peat, mowing grass, and assisting in all the operations of hay-making. They are all blacksmiths also from necessity, and the best shoers of horses on the island. The feet of the Iceland horse would be cut to pieces over the sharp rock and lava, if not well shod. The great resort of the peasantry is the church; and should any of the numerous horses have lost a shoe, or be likely to do so, the priest puts on his apron, lights his little charcoal fire in his smithy (one of which is always attached to every parsonage), and sets the animal on his legs again. And here again he has a laborious task to perform in procuring his charcoal. Whatever the distance may be to the nearest thicket of dwarf birch, he must go thither to burn the wood, and to bring it home when charred, across his horse's back.

"This mode of life, however, may not be considered as altogether consistent with the character of him who is entrusted with the religious instruction of his humble parishioners. Sir George Mackenzie says, that the minister of the Gardé, styled the Provost of Goldbringé Syssel, and superintendent of all the ecclesiastical concerns of that district, was so poor that, to use his own words—'Knowing his poverty, we were not surprised that this dignitary of the Church exhibited in his person and habiliments a figure, the description of which we shall spare our readers, that they may not partake the pain inspired by the most squalid indigence in a clerical garb.' Yet the poor man had a considerable collection of books, and among others translations of some of the works of Pope, and Young's 'Night Thoughts.' Their condition may have, and probably, has a beneficial effect. What an example may it not afford for the poor peasantry to be contented with their lot, many of whom, indeed, are in far better circumstances than those of their pastor! But whether this equality of drudgery and of external habiliments be favourable to the propagation of religion, morality, and of that respect which is due to the sacred character of the pastor, is not for me to offer an opinion; but, taking the whole island, there is little doubt that the pastor and his flock are nearly on an equality as to worldly concerns. None of them can be considered as wealthy, but all of them appear to be contented with their lot; poverty, indeed, may truly be said to be the general condition of the Icelandic inhabitants." (pp. 235-240).

Painful details of the extreme poverty

of the clergy follow, which I pass over. But I cannot deny myself the pleasure of introducing a character of literature and genius, among these exemplary and destitute pastors of the Church, shining out amid the surrounding darkness and wretchedness of indigence and poverty.

"One example shall suffice as an illustration of what has been said respecting the triumph of literary pursuits over pinching penury. It is the case of an Icelandic clergyman, of the name of Jonas Thorlakson, the parish priest of Backa. This venerable pastor, when nearly seventy years of age, had just completed a translation of Milton's 'Paradise Lost,' into his native tongue, having previously translated Pope's 'Essay on Man.' Three of the first books only of the 'Paradise Lost' were printed by the Icelandic Society, when it was dissolved in 1796, and to print the rest at his own expense was altogether out of the question, as we are told that the whole of his annual income, from the united parishes of Baegisa and Backa, did not exceed thirty-six dollars, or 6*l.* sterling, out of which he had to pay an assistant nearly half.* This must, of course, mean the pittance given by the crown, his parishioners and his glebe making up the rest. In allusion to his poverty, he thus expresses himself in Icelandic verse :—' Ever since I came into the world, I have been wedded to Poverty, who has now hugged me to her bosom these seventy winters, all but two; and whether we shall ever be separated, is only known to Him who has joined us together.'" (pp. 245, 246).

An affecting account of the dwelling of this "venerable man," as he is justly styled, follows these passages.

" This description (continues Mr. Barrow) of the deplorable condition of so superior a genius as Thorlakson unquestionably was, being fully corroborated by enquiries made of Mr. Bourke, then Danish minister at the court of London, was not unheeded by our countrymen." The literary fund granted him 30*l*., equal to five years' income of his miserable pittance. He signed a receipt for the money, as he

* " Journal of a Residence in Iceland," by E. Henderson, vol. i., p. 98.

writes therein—" signed with my own hand," being then in the seventy-third year of his age. He did not long survive this act of benevolence. To show himself, by his attainments, worthy of this benevolent attention of strangers, we are told— " He wrote a letter in very elegant Latin, expressing his heartfelt gratitude for the kindness and generosity of the society, so accordant with the character of the British nation, and accompanied it with a MS. copy of his translation of Milton's 'Paradise Lost,' into the Icelandic language; but the latter is not to be found, being taken away, probably by one of the members, who particularly interested himself in the case, and who is since dead." (pp. 247, 248).

This melancholy instance of the gratitude of an accomplished mind, and of an individual who, in England, would have held a respectable situation in society, brings forcibly to one's memory the touching lines of our great contemporary poet:—

"I've heard of hearts unkind, kind deeds
With coldness still returning;
Alas! the GRATITUDE of men
Has oftener left me mourning."
WORDSWORTH.

One more extract from this interesting work, and I have done.

The Prince of Denmark came to Iceland during the visit of our traveller, and made himself very agreeable, both to the visitors and inhabitants of those northern regions. In Mr. Barrow's final chapter of "Leave-taking" is the following paragraph, on the prospective benefit of this royal visit to Iceland :—

"It is to be hoped that this visit of the prince will have the good effect of being attended with benefit to those who, in all probability, will become his future subjects—indeed, I am confident that he will neither forget nor neglect them. A small addition to the public expenditure of Denmark might be made an important boon to these poor people, *and, above all, to the clergy whose lamentable condition he must have witnessed during his travels.* An addition of ten pounds a year to each of their miserable stipends, which would not entail an increase of three thousand pounds—nay, even half that sum—would bring down the blessings of the whole community on his head." (p. 315).

I could not easily have made less copious extracts from an account of such an exemplary people and clergy, of a sister Church, without doing something like injustice and injury to the cause which I have fervently at heart. The enemies of the Church, in these days, may take occasion, from the perusal of this narrative of the poor circumstances of the clergy of an Episcopal Church, to make an invidious comparison of the situation of the Church in Great Britain, and now, in some degree, in her vast possessions and colonies in the East and West. Such I heed not. But, as a Churchman, I bless God that He has not thought fit to afflict our own beloved country with similarly severe visitations.

But let us look at this singular history in another light. How gracious is that Providence which—amid such physical inconveniences and hardships, such bitter penury and privation of all personal comfort, in a climate so fiercely visited by the opposing elements of fire and cold—raises up a hardy, a contented, and a pious people, a clergy deriving their divine commission from the Apostles, and enduring even more than THEIR poverty! And this society is held together, and trained up for the society of the saints in light hereafter, amid circumstances almost incredibly adverse.

It proves to us another consolatory fact, that when the time comes, if come it must, that "the candle of the Lord" shall cease to send forth her wonted light from the altars of our own beloved Church, and we, in turn, shall be doomed to have our candlestick removed, or at least to suffer great temporal afflictions, we have before our eyes, in the clergy and laity of these poor, pious, and patient Icelanders, a living monument of what can be endured by the humble professors and ministers of the pure Catholic and Apostolic Church of Christ.

The Church of Christ was designed by its Divine Founder to mould itself to all circumstances—and, in the words of the great Apostle to the Gentiles, to be " all things to all men, so that she may gain some." In remote parts of Sweden and Norway, in Lapland and Finland, and in Iceland, we see how she may subsist amid external poverty and penury. In a part of our own island, in Scotland, a portion of the same Church has subsisted, in spite of persecution and poverty, ever since the establishment of Presbytery: and, though much improved in her outward circumstances, she is still in a state of considerable depression. But in England she yet stands firm and unshaken by the storm. She " spreads out her boughs unto the sea, and her branches unto the river."

Almost every year, for sometime past, she has sent forth new bishops and accessions of clergy to her distant colonies. Her rank is high in a temporal sense, as it ought to be, in a wealthy and powerful empire, such as Great Britain and Ireland. For the same reason why, in such a state of melancholy and depression as that of Iceland, the clergy are *no higher* than the people, certainly in such a splendid empire as our own they should not be *lower*. They ought, as they do in our bishops, dignitaries, and working clergy, to mix freely and almost equally, with every rank and gradation of the people. SUCH IS THE UNITED CHURCH OF ENGLAND AND IRELAND. LONG MAY SHE SO CONTINUE! WOE UNTO ENGLAND WHEN OF THE CHURCH IT MAY BE SAID, THAT "HER PLACE KNOWS HER NO MORE!"*

* See Supplement, No. IV.

Note I, Page 34.

THE OVERTHROW OF EPISCOPACY IN SCOTLAND.

The following extract from another of the excellent works of the THEOLOGICAL LIBRARY—by a well-known learned and accomplished writer, the Right Reverend Dr. Michael Russell, the author of the "Sacred and Profane History," in the interval between Shuckford and Prideaux, now Bishop of Glasgow (whom the writer is proud to number among his friends)—will abundantly illustrate what is briefly said in the text respecting the Reformation in Scotland, the overthrow of Episcopacy, and the final establishment of Presbyterianism, contrary to the wishes of the mass of the people. Bishop Russell's work had long been a desideratum in Ecclesiastical History, and it could not have fallen into abler hands to fill up the blank.

"During the whole reign of King William, indeed, the Episcopalians, owing to their supposed bias in favour of the older dynasty, were much discountenanced in Scotland, and their clergy subjected to many hardships; but, as has been already mentioned, the greater part of the nobility and landholders of ancient families continued strongly attached to that form of ecclesiastical polity, and afforded them both support and protection. In the northern counties, we are assured, the preference for Episcopacy was so strong, that little regard was paid to the Presbyterian courts; and the ministers who kept their kirks, being shielded by the gentry and beloved by the people, seldom or never appeared before these new tribunals. In some parishes, where the old patrons were the principal proprietors, and thereby had influence over the inhabitants, the vacant churches were filled with clergymen who had received Episcopal ordination, either from the bishop of the diocese, or from some other, whose residence was less distant. The result, viewed as affecting the body at large, was more singular than gratifying to either party; presenting the spectacle of a national Church, which, in strict language, was neither Presbyterian nor Episcopal, but a heterogeneous compound of two jarring denominations; both of them publicly acknowledged to be ministers of the Gospel, invested with pastoral charges, and formally confirmed by legal authority, though they were not in full communion with each other, nor agreeing in some essential parts of divine worship.

"It cannot have escaped the reader that, both in 1638 and 1688, the Church in Scotland was overthrown by a pressure from without, directed by an active faction, and influenced by political motives. In the former case, the clergy were not allowed to choose their own delegates to represent them in the General Assembly, because it was known that a great majority of them were friendly to the Episcopal form of government; while at the era of the Revolution, the countenance of the State was withdrawn, because the bishops could not, without being allowed time for due reflection, consent to transfer their allegiance from one sovereign to another. On this occasion also the parochial incumbents throughout the greater part of the kingdom were averse to the change—a remark which may be perhaps extended to the people, except in the disturbed districts, where the principles of the Covenant had taken a deeper root."*

The second extract will show the ruinous effects of the Act of Parliament passed after the Rebellion of 1745, not so much by persecution of the Episcopalians by the fanatical Presbyterians, which was sufficiently cruel, as by the Act of Pains and Penalties, respecting the worship of this pure and primitive Church, which was not repealed until the year 1792. I have heard

---

* "The statements of Episcopal writers on this subject must, no doubt, be received with some caution; but they are unanimous in asserting that, except in the confederated counties, the great body of the people was with them. Alluding to the 'inclinations of the people' on which the Presbyterian establishment was avowedly founded, the author of the 'Fundamental Charter' maintains, that such inclinations could not be collected from any clamour made at that time against prelacy by the generality of the people; there were no such clamours in the mouths of the *twentieth part* of the people. They could not collect them from the people's separation from the Episcopal clergy during the time of King James's toleration: the *tenth part* of the nation had not separated. Is it reasonable to judge of a *whole kingdom by a corner of it*—to call those the sentiments of *all* the kingdom which were only the sentiments of four or five counties?" (pp. 297-299).

a venerable bishop of that Church, who would have done honour to any Church (my own revered father-in-law, Bishop Gleig, the late Primus), more than once declare, very emphatically, that those severe penal laws did not so much suppress Episcopacy, as that they suppressed Christianity itself. I have, moreover, heard it attested by sensible Scotchmen, who well knew their own ecclesiastical history, that many of the most influential families in the country, who could not attend their own pastors, and would not go to the churches of the Presbyterian establishment, gradually ceased to attend any place of worship whatever. Thus many of the descendants of those, who once were pious Churchmen, became infidels; and hence, perhaps, combined with other causes intimately associated with the peculiar doctrine and discipline of the Genevan Reformer, the notorious prevalence, at the end of the last and the beginning of the present century, of infidelity.

"The injury done to the Episcopal Church in Scotland by the persecution of the clergy would not probably have been great, or of very long duration, had it not extended likewise to the laity of that communion. But the Act further declared, that if, after the first of September, any person should resort to an illegal Episcopal meeting-house, and not give information, within five days of such meeting, to some proper magistrate, he should be subjected to fine or imprisonment. It declared further, that no peer of Scotland should be capable of being elected one of the sixteen peers of Parliament, or of voting at such election; and that no person should be capable of being elected a member of Parliament for any shire or borough, or of voting at such election, who should, within the compass of a year, have been twice present at any Episcopal meeting in Scotland, not held according to law. In this state of things some of those clergymen who, though zealous Episcopalians, had always professed themselves not Jacobites, feeling it their duty to render their chapels legal meeting-houses, repaired to the proper magistrates, took the oaths required by the Act, and had their letters of orders registered before the 1st day of September.

But this compliance availed them nothing, for in May, 1748, the former statute was amended, when it was declared, 'that no letters of orders not granted by some bishop of the Church of England or Ireland, should, after the 22nd of September, be sufficient to qualify any pastor or minister of any Episcopal meeting in Scotland, whether the same had been registered before or since the 1st of September, 1746; and that every such registration, whether made before or since, should be null and void.'

"This Act, it is manifest, was directly levelled against the religion of Scottish Episcopalians, for it precluded them from the privilege of political repentance. As such it was felt by the English bishops, not one of whom would support the bill; while some of them, as Sherlock, Secker, and Maddox, spoke strenuously against it, as a flagrant attack on the leading principles of Christian liberty. The amendment, however, as it was called, passed in the Commons with little opposition; but in the House of Peers it required great management on the part of Lord Chancellor Hardwicke, who, after all his exertions, could not secure more than a majority of five. By this severe statute the complying clergymen were subjected to the very same persecution which those endured who refused to take the oaths and to name the sovereign in their prayers. Some of them were imprisoned; others sought shelter by crossing the Tweed; while a great number left their native country altogether, and endeavoured to find freedom of worship, and the means of supporting their families, in the colonies of North America.

"There is not to be found, in any Protestant nation, an example of penal laws at once so oppressive and insidious as those of which the history has now been described. A resolution was thereby avowed to extirpate a whole communion, by rendering their worship illegal, and by depriving them of all the political privileges which are most highly valued in a free country. In less enlightened times, when death was made the punishment of an erring faith, public sympathy was in general so much excited that the bloodiest statutes were soon reduced to a dead letter. Even in Scotland, where the influence of public opinion was probably less felt than in any other European kingdom, the attempt made to check the Reformation involved the sacrifice of but few lives, whether in civil or ecclesiastical courts. The sight of a martyr, standing amidst the faggots which are about to consume his living flesh, creates deep thoughts and serious reflections in all who witness his constancy; and hence, in most cases, the cause which has recourse to such means for support has rushed to a speedy and irretrievable fall. But who compassionated the unseen prisoner and the weary exile? Who traced the steps or the sufferings of him who was chased from the scene of his Christian labours, saw his chapel closed, his flocked scattered, his person reviled, and the sources of an honest independence dried up?

"Law pursued him on the form of starvation and contempt, marking him as one excluded from the benefits of civil society, deprived of political rights himself, and carrying a similar disqualification to others. Even his meek resignation and unresisting principles exposed him to neglect; for had he, like the Covenanter, taken the field and sounded the note of war, he would have assumed a more interesting attitude in the public eye, and his death on the scaffold would at least have thrown a deeper odium on an illiberal government.

"The privations which the Scottish Episcopalians were doomed to endure are recorded no where, except in those private histories, the materials of which belong to biography, rather than to a general narrative. All appearance of public worship was necessarily avoided, and the clergy had recourse to a method, practised by them before they enjoyed toleration, of visiting families in private, where a few faithful followers met to celebrate the rites of their Church in the utmost secrecy.* Sometimes they had little chapels, if such they might be called, in the recesses of narrow streets or alleys, where they convened the more resolute of their adherents with caution, and by stealth. Frequently these secluded places of worship were in the lofts of ruined stables and cow-houses, and were only approachable by moveable ladders and trap-doors, placed under the charge of some vigilant friend; and at one time the existence of such retreats was carefully concealed, except from those in whom the greatest reliance could be reposed. At the present day, the traveller in one part of Scotland may visit the wild caves in which the heroes of the Covenant shunned the pursuit

* "Many did duty on the same Sunday sixteen several times, to keep within the terms of the law."

of Claverhouse and Dalziel; and in another, especially in the towns beyond the Forth, he may see the rude garrets and antiquated apartments wherein, during their period of dejection, were wont to assemble a few concealed worshippers belonging to the Scottish Episcopal Church. For the latter no indulgence appeared, and to them no terms of accommodation were ever held out; and the fact that their communion was not utterly extinguished before forty-two years of such darkness passed away, can only be ascribed to the power of principle co-operating with the sense of duty."*—*History of the Church in Scotland.* By the Right Rev. Bishop Russell. In 2 vols. London. 1834. Vol. ii., pp. 381-383, 402-406.

The reader may consult Dr. Coote's con-

* "Book of Scotland," p. 462. In the register of the Episcopal Chapel at Muthill is the following entry after a baptism, under March 20th, 1750:—"N.B. With such excessive severity were the penal laws executed at this thime, that Andrew Moir having neglected to keep his appointment with me at my own house this morning, and following me to Lord Rollo's house, of Duncoub, we could not take the child into a house, but I was obliged to go under the cover of the trees in one of Lord Rollo's parks, to prevent our being discovered, and baptize the child there."

tinuation of Mosheim's "Ecclesiastical History" (vol. vi., p. 299) respecting those facts. But the notice is very brief. See the same, p. 337, for the consecration of Dr. Seabury, the first bishop of the Episcopal Church of the United States of America, by the bishops of the Scotch Episcopal Church, in the year 1784. A similar event, in the consecration of the Right Reverend Bishop Luscombe, of Paris, occurred in 1825; and it was upon his consecration that Dr. Hook delivered the admirable sermon, which he afterwards published, and from which I have already made some extracts (see ante, note H). In the advertisement to this discourse a brief sketch is given of the history of the present Episcopal Church in Scotland.

NOTE K, PAGE 53.

BISHOP HORNE'S OPINION OF THE SCOTCH EPISCOPAL CHURCH.

The prelate referred to is Bishop Horne. The passage was written from memory, and is so inserted. The anecdote is related in "The Life of Bishop Horne," by the Rev. William Jones, of Nayland. I subjoin the entire passage, which is too interesting to be omitted:—

"From the present circumstances of its primitive orthodoxy, piety, poverty, and depressed state, he had such an opinion of this Church, as to think that, if the great Apostle of the Gentiles were upon earth, and it were put to his choice with what denomination of Christians he would communicate, the preference would probably be given to the Episcopalians of Scotland, as most like to the people he had been used to. This happened, as I perfectly recollect, while we were talking together on the subject of the Scotch petition, on one of the hills near the city of Canterbury, higher than the pinnacles of the Cathedral, where there was no witness to our discourse but the sky that was over our heads; and yet, when all things are duly considered, I think no good man would have been angry if he had overheard us."

Bishop Horne was a zealous friend of the Scottish Episcopalians, when, in 1791, they applied to Parliament to repeal the Act of Pains and Penalties of 1746. The following anecdote is related by Jones:—

"It was said, about this time, that the Lord Chancellor Thurlow withheld his consent to the Scotch Episcopal Bill, till he should be satisfied by some of the English prelates that there really were bishops in Scotland. When Bishop Horne was waited upon with this view of the committee of the Scotch Church, and one of them observed that his lordship could assure the Chancellor they were *good bishops*, he answered, with his usual affability and good humour, 'Yes, sir, much better bishops than I am.'

"A clergyman of Scotland, who had received English ordination, applied to him, wishing to be considered as under the jurisdiction of some English bishop; that is, to be, in effect, independent of the bishops of Scotland in their own country; but he gave no countenance to the proposal, and advised the person who made it quietly to acknowledge the bishop of the diocese in which he lived, who he knew would be ready to receive him into communion, and require nothing of him but what was necessary to maintain the order and unity of a Christian Church; assuring him, at the same time, that, if he were a private clergyman himself, he should be glad to be under the authority of such a bishop."—*Jones's Life of Dr. Horne.* Theological Works, vol. vi., pp. 140-141. London, 1810.

Note L, Page 37.

UNIVERSALITY OF THE CATHOLIC CHURCH.

"The office and character of all persons who are admitted into holy orders extends over the whole world; and it is manifest, in the first place, that the Apostles had a general commission to *teach and baptize,* and to execute all other parts of their office, in *all nations.* And as the *bishops* of the Church have been shown to succeed the *Apostles,* in all the parts of their office which are of standing and constant use in the Church; so we might reasonably conclude, though we had no further proof of it, that the office and character of *bishops,* and consequently of inferior ministers, extends over all the world, because those of the *Apostles* their predecessors, did so; since there is scarce any reason why the *Apostles'* authority should be universal, which will not hold, at least in some degrees, for the same extent of authority in the *bishops;* as will appear from some of the following considerations.

"There is but one Catholic Church, whereof all particular Churches are members; and therefore, when any spiritual privilege or character is conferred in any particular Church, it must be understood to extend over the whole Catholic Church. Thus by baptism men are not only made members of the particular Church where they happen to be baptized, but of the Catholic Church over the whole world; and therefore, whoever has been lawfully baptized in one Church, has a right to partake of the Lord's Supper, and other Church privileges, in all other churches where he happens to come: whereas if baptism only admitted men into some particular Churches, they must be re-baptized before they can lawfully be received to communion in any diocese where they have not been baptized already.

"If it were not thus in holy orders, that they who have received them in one place retain them in others, no minister could have authority to preach the Gospel, or to administer the sacraments, or to exercise any other part of his function, beyond the particular district in which he was ordained. The consequence whereof is manifestly this, that the faith of Christ must not be propagated, nor any churches erected, in countries where they have not stood ever since the *Apostles'* times. For since there can be no ministers without ordination, as was before proved, either they who have been ordained in one country may lawfully exercise their respective functions in others, where there are no ordained ministers already settled, or else these countries must remain for ever without ministers, and consequently without sacraments, and other public offices of religion.

"It is manifest that the offices of those ministers whom the *Apostles* ordained were not confined to any certain place or church: for we find that *Timothy, Titus, Crescens,* and others who are spoken of in the *Acts* and *Epistles,* travelled with *St. Paul* and other *Apostles,* and sometimes without them, and exercised their ministerial functions in very distant parts of the world. In the next age after them, *Polycarp, St. John's* disciple, and *Bishop* of Smyrna, travelled to *Rome,* where Anicetus, the *bishop* of that city, *out of respect to him, desired him to consecrate the Eucharist;* whereas, if *Polycarp's* sacerdotal character had extended no farther than his own diocese of Smyrna, he must have been re-ordained at *Rome* before he could consecrate there. And for the same reason, whoever was justly excommunicated by his own *bishop*, was held excommunicated all over the world."—*A Discourse of Church Government.* By Archbishop Potter. pp. 443-445. London, 1707. 8vo.

Note M, Page 37.

THE FREE CONSTITUTION OF THE CHURCH.

Among the calumnies which in this age are heaped upon the Church of England — besides her alleged intolerance and worldliness, from which, as a whole, she is more free than any other Christian community—her *tyranny* is very commonly insisted on by her enemies. Nothing can involve a greater and a more wilful error than this charge. As it regards the bishops and clergy, her government is emphatically *paternal*. It admits not of coercion beyond the known law, which alone is tyranny. The people or laity of our Church enjoy a more perfect freedom of conscience and liberal toleration than those of any other church or sect. Nor can the bishops exercise tyranny over the inferior clergy. The presbyters are a free body, giving willing obedience to their superiors in all things lawful; but if the bishop, which is rarely or never the case, should be tempted to outstep the prescribed limits of his authority, the presbyters would be the first to check and oppose him.

The Church is governed by the written or canon law, and by custom or tradition; which answers to the common law of the nation at large. Were our Houses of Convocation restored, this freedom of the Church within itself would be apparent to all. The rights of the entire Church, as it is composed of the people and the clergy, would be better understood. I have somewhere met with the remark, that perhaps the free Parliaments of Europe, of which the freedom of the British Parliament is most conspicuous, may have taken their rise from the synods and convocations of the Church. This, however, is not important. Respecting the early synods of the Church the following extracts from a modern periodical work may suffice:—

"Assemblies of the clergy appear to have been held very frequently from the beginning of Christianity, under the heathen emperors, as we are informed by Eusebius, Cyprian, and Tertullian. The necessity for such assemblies, even in the earliest periods of the Church, is self-evident. During the life-time of the Apostles, when the Church was governed by holy men who spake under the immediate inspiration of God, we find questions of discipline arising among the disciples of Christianity, which required for their decision the assembling of themselves together. How much more frequently, then, would such questions occur at an after period, when the extraordinary gifts of the Spirit had departed?

The earliest assemblies of the clergy were composed of the bishops and presbyters, who were seated, and of the deacons and people, who stood before them, and who were little more than witnesses of what passed in the synod. The presbyters, indeed, in every city, formed a necessary standing council to their respective bishop, and, together with the bishop, formed a diocesan synod, in which they met to give their advice and consent upon all important matters."

Speaking of other synods, whereof the inferior clergy were members, with equal powers of deliberation with the other members, this writer proceeds :—

"The constitutions passed in those synods always ran in the name, and were stated to be passed with the consent and approbation, of the inferior clergy, even when they were only represented by the archdeacons, to whom they had given procuratorial instruments. Thus in the Council of Merton, 42 H. 3, the constitutions which were there made, are stated to have passed ' de unanimi assensu et consilio prælatorum religiosorum, et totius cleri ecclesiæ ;' and towards the end the same form is repeated in a still more clear and detailed manner:—'Archiepiscopi et episcopi de consensu et approbatione inferiorum prælatorum capitulorum, cathedralium, et conventualium, necnon universitatis totius cleri Angliæ hæc prædicta communiter et concorditer providerunt.'"—*Church of England Quarterly Review* for January, 1839, pp. 62, 63, vol. v.

Note N, Page 52.

BISHOPS MIDDLETON AND HEBER.

From this bright array of names of Christian heroes, who have fearlessly stood up and boldly contended for the TRUTH as it is in JESUS, " and the FAITH once delivered to the saints," it is scarcely possible for the true lover of his Church, and an ordained clergyman of that Church serving in an Indian diocese, not to select BISHOP MIDDLETON.

I have styled this eminently learned and high-minded prelate "the first and the greatest glory of Christian India." So I esteem him. In saying this do I depreciate from the pious labours and character of other eminent prelates who have succeeded him in office and have not fallen behind him in zeal, and from the exemplary clergy who participated in his elevated views, and co-operated with this first great prelate in the glorious work of establishing and diffusing true and vital religion in and over the empire of British India? God forbid. Do I forget the highly gifted, and, as he has been styled, with a pardonable hyperbole, the " seraphic" Heber, of whom, if of any one, as respected his lamented and premature death, it may be said, in the pathetic language of poetry—

" The good die first:
And they, whose hearts are dry as summer's dust,
Burn to the socket?"

Do I disparage the pious labours and the fervent zeal of the prelates who now fill the Episcopal sees of India? No; I cherish rather a strong hope and a confident anticipation that the Divine Providence will raise up, as the wants of the Church may indicate, new Middletons and new Hebers! I would, however, at the same time, remind both the clergy and the laity of the Church in India of the vast labours and of the painful difficulties that still surround our bishops, and beset their path at every step. I would conjure them, by the love of Christ, and by their veneration for His holy Catholic Church, to rally round the Episcopal chair in this age of schism and Dissent, when the fathers of the Church are fiercely assailed by men who perversely think they do God service by their attempt to lower His ministers, the bishops of the Church. Let *us* especially, of this diocese of Madras, faithfully and affectionately support our own beloved bishop, who is in no measure exempted from the trials and difficulties of his revered predecessors in his and their high and holy office.

Bishops Middleton and Heber were sen

forth by the all-wise providence of God under very trying circumstances, and at very peculiar seasons of the Church. The life of Bishop Middleton was truly that of an Apostle—full of labours and difficulties, under which even his powerful mind at last sank. He was over-wrought and over-excited. The sword was too highly tempered; it pierced the scabbard: the mortal tabernacle gave way. A less energetic mind would have been later over-tasked. Like the robust Luther, Middleton cleared the pathways of obstructions; while, like the milder Melancthon, the amiable Heber spread the waters over the plain.* Yet this was too full of labour and excitement. He fell in two short years. Middleton, by a rare combination of powers, had sustained his gigantic struggle for almost nine years.

As an author, Bishop Middleton stands

---

* Some such saying is recorded of Luther himself respecting his brother Reformer, the mild and amiable Melancthon. What high honour does it reflect on both these great men!

at the head of his age. His "Doctrine of the Greek Article" cut up by the roots the Socinian, rather the *Unitarian*, heresy. Archbishop Magee, another giant in this holy war, appeals continually, in his elaborate work on the Atonement, to this deeply learned performance of the great Indian bishop. In one part, if my memory be correct, for I cannot find the passage, he recommends it to the theological student as his inseparable companion. "Nocturnâ versate manu, versate diurnâ."

One passage, however, I beg to cite, as decisive of the esteem of Dr. Magee for this great biblical critic and classical scholar.

The archbishop refutes, in his forcible manner and style, the heretical glosses of the Unitarian critics on the scriptural phrase of "the Son of God," and "the Son of Man." He concludes the paragraph in these words:—

"For a full and satisfactory explanation of the force of the phrase 'Son of Man,' and especially in its application in John v. 27; and for the reason why the Greek Article is here omitted, which is found to accompany the title wherever else it occurs throughout the Gospels, I refer to a critic who had well considered, and had taken pains thoroughly to understand, the subject, before he submitted his opinions to the public—Dr. Middleton. (*Doctrine of the Greek Article*, pp. 351-354). The title 'Son of Man,' he observes justly, ' has everywhere a reference to the incarnation of Christ:' and he adds, that generally, in the use of the application by our Lord, ' the allusion is either to His present humiliation or to His future glory:' and therefore, he concludes, we have in this phrase, though an indirect, yet a strong and perpetual declaration, that the human nature did not originally belong to Him, and was not properly His own."—*Discourses upon the Atonement, &c.* By Archbishop Magee. 4th edit., vol. ii., part 2, p. 494. London, 1816.

The other writings of Bishop Middleton, published by Archdeacon Bonney, consisting of charges and sermons, are not numerous; and as by his will he peremptorily ordered all his manuscript writings to be destroyed, we must rest satisfied with what remains of this mighty mind. Yet we cannot but regret that "such things were, and were most precious," since they are for ever lost to us. It were scarcely possible, indeed, that anything which fell from Bishop Middleton's pen could be without considerable value.

His Life, by Mr. Le Bas, and his admirable letters interspersed through that interesting work, present us with the portrait of a man who was worthy to have been the first bishop of India, and the founder of Bishop's College, Calcutta. It is singular that both Bishops Middleton and Heber at first declined, with unfeigned humility, the great undertaking of being the head of the Church in India. Both subsequently accepted the office, from the superior sense of duty. It is impossible to suspect such men of any but the highest and the purest motives: both may be said to have laid down their lives for the faith.

I cannot but extract, in this note, Bishop Middleton's rules, drawn up before he left

England, for his future guidance—"So full (says Mr. Le Bas) of admirable good sense, that his biography would be incomplete without their insertion." They are as follow:—

"Invoke divine aid—Preach frequently, and as 'one having authority'—Promote schools, charities, literature, and good taste—Nothing great can be accomplished without policy—Persevere against discouragement—Keep your temper—Employ leisure in study, and always have some work in hand—Be punctual and methodical in business, and never procrastinate—Keep up a close connexion with friends at home—Attend to forms—Never be in a hurry—Preserve self-possession, and do not be talked out of conviction—Rise early, and be an economist of time—Maintain dignity, without the appearance of pride: manner is something with everybody, and everything with some—Be guarded in discourse, attentive, and slow to speak—Never acquiesce in immoral or pernicious opinions—Beware of concessions and pledges—Be not forward to assign reasons to those who have no right to demand them—Be not subservient nor timid in manner, but manly and independent, firm and decided—

Think nothing in conduct unimportant and indifferent—Be of no party—Be popular, if possible, but at any rate be respected—Remonstrate against abuses, where there is any chance of correcting them—Advise and encourage youth—Rather set than follow example—Observe a grave economy in domestic affairs—Practice strict temperance—Remember what is expected in England—And lastly—Remember the final account."

"Such (continues his biographer) were the golden maxims by which the first Protestant bishop of India proposed to regulate his steps through the arduous region of usefulness now opening before him; and such were the thoughts and occupations by which the tedious interval of his voyage was converted into a season of preparation for future sacrifices and exertions."—*Le Bas' Life of Bishop Middleton*, vol. i., p. 60.

The Rev. Charles Forster, the biographer of his eminent friend, the late Bishop Jebb, thus writes of the first Bishop of Calcutta :—

" It is my duty to subjoin the testimony of a

name, already venerable in the history of our Church, as a happy example of the compatibility of much learning and deep scholarship, with almost apostolic zeal and labours. The reader may possibly anticipate the name of BISHOP MIDDLETON."—*Forster's Life of Bishop Jebb.* Second edition, pp. 151, 152.

The private letters of eminent men are justly prized. They admit us into " the business and bosoms" of superior minds. They often contain, incidentally, the finest traits of character, and the purest sentiments. I cannot refuse myself the gratification of quoting one extract from one of the many admirable letters of Bishop Middleton to his intimate friend, and I believe distant relation, Mr. Seth Ward, to whom he unfolds the kindliest and the most natural feelings of the human heart. This extract, elevated by a lofty piety, is of this character. I quote it, too, as will be seen, from a motive somewhat personal. To this beloved friend, soon after his arrival in India, he thus expresses himself:—

"I often reflect with wonder on the ways of Providence, when I consider my own extraordinary life. But four years since I quitted my peaceful retreat on the banks of Nen, where any small degree of energy natural to me was nearly laid to rest, and I never read the service at the altar of Tansor Church without the thought coming across me that I was standing on the spot where my remains would probably repose. My sphere of duty was very humble, and the improvement which honest farmer Cave used to declare he derived from my sermons was the most valuable reward of my labours."—*Le Bas' Life*, vol. i., p. 158.

The wonderful ways of Providence, perhaps, in one man's life, were never more visibly displayed than in that of this distinguished prelate. In reference to the subject of the above extract, I cannot but wonder at the ways of Providence even with regard to the limited sphere in which it is my own lot to move. In my early life I well knew the scene of the bishop's little rectory on the banks of the river Nen.

I was, at the beginning of the present century, educated at the foundation school about two miles from the little village of Tansor. The rural church on the bank of the river; the little thatched rectory, or cottage, on the opposite side of the road, looking upon the river and the meadows beyond it; the very figure of farmer Cave, whom I familiarly knew—all these pleasing yet melancholy images of home and of boyhood rise up freshly before my mind's eye at this instant, when, labouring in my humble vocation, I am placed, by the same benign Providence, in a remote island, which once was in the diocese, and is now in the province, of Calcutta. Here, too, I perhaps may fall, without even "the shadow of a name." Yet in recalling all these images, I almost feel with the poet, on revisiting his native country—

"Vix mî ipse credens, Thyanium atque Bithynos Liquisse campos."

Note O, Page 58.

THE TRUE SPIRIT OF THE CHURCH OF ENGLAND.

" Without a clear apprehension of the theological scale, and the graduations marked upon it, not only much outward activity may be misspent, but plans of Providence, even those that have been carried on from century to century, may be misconceived and undervalued. Institutions, invaluable with respect to true essentials, may be lightly esteemed, because they have no aptitude to other matters erroneously thought important. While, on the other hand, an overrating of non-essentials will naturally make those things which support them—men, books, or practices—be overrated also; till at length a fallacy is discovered, and then, too probably, follows a rejection as indiscriminate as was the preference before. I conceive we have been long witnessing the first of these results, in the numberless secessions, within the last thirty or forty years, from the Establishment; and the latter result is too sure to occur whenever reason is disposed to assume supreme authority, after its temporary displacement.

"Is there anything in all this? If there be, a remedy is to be looked for; and what is that remedy? I think God himself has given it, through Jeremiah. I have said something like it already; but as it stands in the prophet, it is decisive: 'Thus saith the Lord; stand ye in the ways and see; and ask for the old paths, where is the good way; and walk therein, and ye shall find rest unto your soul.' What, then, are, with respect to us, the old paths? Not surely those paths which are not yet three centuries old. Whatever there be of this kind, is not old, but new. When fifteen centuries lie beyond, to be traversed, we must make our way into these, and rise high in them, before we can be sure of having what has really stood the test of time: and when in such a research we find deep substantial agreement, even the darkest age not wholly without its luminaries, and the luminaries of all the successive ages uniting in one testimony to a few radical truths, and in one harmonious expression of that piety, purity, and charity, of which those truths, received in the love of them, were the seeds and elements—than such Catholicity what on this earth can be more satisfying to the mind, or more influential on the heart?

"This, I venture to assert, is the true spirit of the Church of England. Had she intended to have made her children either Lutherans or Calvinists, she would have harmonized her formularies in conformity with such an object. But in retaining the ancient forms with such scrupulous care, she has taught us to go, for further satisfaction, to the same quarter. This steady retention was, of all the acts of our Church, the most radical and solemn, and, of course, the most characteristic. It tells us, therefore, that we are no further true members of the Church of England, than as we are, in the justest and strictest sense, Catholic; that is, diligent enquirers after the united sense of the regular Christian Church (interpreting holy Scripture), and steady adherents to what we thus find clearly avouched to us. This is what the Church of England took as its own leading principle, in subordination solely to the self-evident light of Scripture: and this it consequently enjoins on all its individual members.

"I fear by this time you will be tired of my talk, and that you will either think me unintelligible, or making much ado about nothing. If such should be your feeling, I could not at once say to you, as I might to very many, 'Lay down my letter, and trouble yourself no more about it:' I should rather beg a reconsideration; at the same time pointing your attention to other facts. Look, for example, how very generally the Nonconformists of England, after the subsidence of puritanic piety, became Arians or Socinians. Look, also, how the descendants of the German pietists have diverged into semi-deism; and observe how widely the leaven of false doctrine has diffused itself through the Calvinistic Church of Scotland.* Attend, lastly, to the controversy at this day within the Church of England, about the meaning of the Thirty-nine Articles, and the obligation incurred by subscription. See how some make absolutely nothing of this or of them, turning the Articles into a dead letter, and assent and consent into a farce; while others would pin down subscribers to all the dogmas of a particular party. Does not this last fact prove us also unsettled? And do not the other facts give evidence of that in which unsettledness is likely to end?"—*Letter to Mrs. Hannah More. Remains of Alexander Knox, Esq.*, vol. iv., pp. 238-241. London, 1837.

* See post, Note R.

Note P, Page 58.

RELIGIOUS OPINIONS OF SAXONY, PRUSSIA, AND GERMANY, DURING THE EIGHTEENTH CENTURY.

"In Saxony and the Prussian territories the metaphysical philosophy of Wolff, Privy Councillor to Frederic William, King of Prussia, had a considerable effect in the diffusion of a sceptical spirit; and, although he was publicly censured for his pernicious writings, and deprived of a professorship at Halle, he continued to propagate his sentiments after his retreat into the principality of Hesse-Cassel. He was subsequently protected by the Swedish court, but was more particularly favoured by that philosophic prince who became King of Prussia in the year 1740. Professor Kant, the celebrated metaphysician, was patronized by the same monarch; and his system likewise tended to generate scepticism.

"This prince, the well-known Frederic, was fond of free enquiry, and eager to evince his superiority to what he considered as idle prejudice. He, therefore, easily suffered himself to be persuaded, by infidel philosophers, that religion was the invention of interested hypocrites and artful statesmen. He was not more favourable in this respect to Christianity than to the Moslem creed. Priests of all persuasions were, in his eye, either wilful deluders of the multitude, or the credulous instruments of delusion. These opinions he gloried in propagating among his friends; and his court thus became the seat of irreligion and a school of impiety. It was a matter of indifference to such a monarch what religion his subjects professed, or whether they followed any religion at all, provided they were subservient to his military and political despotism. He considered the morality of different sects as nearly the same;* and while he tolerated all, his active vigilance kept his dominions in tranquillity, undisturbed by open animosities or serious dissensions. His people were free in a religious sense, but in no other respect.

"Societies of *illuminati*, or enlightened reasoners, were at length formed in some of the Protestant towns and principalities of Germany, and even in several of the [Roman] Catholic States. At Munich, Professor Weishaupt, who had received his education among the Jesuits,

* "Il n'y a aucune religion (he said) qui, sur le sujet de la morale, s'ecarte beaucoup des autres."

became the founder of a club of reformists; and when he had been banished from Bavaria for his dangerous principles, he was protected and encouraged by the Duke of Saxe-Gotha. Baron Knigge strenuously laboured in the same cause; and, although greater effects have been attributed to these societies than their real importance may induce us to believe, it must be allowed that they paved the way for revolutionary mischief, and aided the pernicious influence of Gallic impiety and sedition."—*Continuation of Mosheim's Ecclesiastical History*, vol. vi., pp. 288-290.

NOTE Q, PAGE 59.

PRESENT STATE OF RELIGION IN GERMANY AND PRUSSIA.

The following extracts are from the work of a recent traveller in Germany. Speaking of Germany generally, he gives the following melancholy account of the state of religion :—

" The truth, however, is—and the theological treatises which issue daily from the German press may satisfy the most incredulous on that head—that a sober and enlightened piety, a firm, and conscientious, and humble belief in the religion of the Gospel, as it was once delivered to the saints, is scarcely professed by any influential portion of the German community. In the [Roman] Catholic countries you find, indeed, some show of respect for the forms of the Church, while [Roman] Catholic divines are, for obvious reasons, less prone to theorize on points of doctrine than Protestants. But even in [Roman] Catholic countries the cloven foot of scepticism is for ever thrusting itself from beneath the priest's robe; while among the Protestants, to believe God's word as it is written forms the exception to the general rule which rationalism has established.

"I have ventured to describe all this when referring to the state of morals and religion in Prussia, and endeavoured to show that a denial of the vital principles of the Gospel necessarily produces extreme laxity in the moral conduct. Let it not be supposed that my remarks apply exclusively to the kingdom of Prussia.

"The following extract, from one of the most influential periodicals of the day, will show that everywhere throughout Germany the same melancholy spirit prevails, and that they who take the lead in the direction of public opinion are not ashamed to avow their subjection to it. 'Christianity with us (says the able writer) seems to stand pretty much in the position of heathenism in the days of Hadrian. As foreign gods were in those days eagerly adopted from all parts of the world, and the countless population of Rome ran after the worship of Egyptian and Syrian idols in rivalry; as the learned found amusement in accommodating their several systems to whatever system of philosophy might chance to be in fashion; so the Christians of Germany now hover in uncertainty about every different confession of religion that occurs, and generally end without adhering to any. The [Roman] Catholics take the lead in the progress of modern enlightenment, and become as sober and rational as Protestants; the Protestants begin to apprehend that they have gone too far, and, distrusting the right of private judgment, publicly coquet with [Roman] Catholic opinions and [Roman] Catholic forms. The differences between Lutheran and Reformed are no more mentioned. A swarm of poets and philosophers from Northern Germany, Protestants by lineage, having made a pilgrimage into the [Roman] Catholic world, become there the most unbending of Ultramontanists, and lead the crusade against their former brethren. While among the [Roman] Catholics an anti-celibatist party has arisen, between whom and the Protestants there exists no essential difference. Then we have fashionable philosophies succeeding one another, or existing together in perfect harmony; and all so flexible that they can, in turn, be adapted to the favourite religious creed of the hour, just as easily as they can be made instruments each for the erection of its own religion. And in the midst of all this confusion the mass of the people are content to rest in indifference, wisely concluding that, where one thing is as good as another, it is best to abide by the religion of their fathers.'—*Literatur Blatt,* Nov. 7, 1836.

" I could quote many passages from others of the literary journals, all of them illustrative of a similar conviction on the part of the writers; but why should I? The controversies which have raged in Germany ever since the appearance of Strauss's " Life of Jesus,"* abundantly bear me out in the views which I have taken;

* The Christology of this new Pantheistic system is elaborately and learnedly refuted by Dr. Mill, in

for even those who object to the author's doctrines are loud in praise of his ingenuity; while not a few ground their objections to this book rather on the method which he has adopted of enforcing and illustrating his opinions, than on the fatal results to which these opinions necessarily lead."—*Germany, Bohemia, and Hungary, visited in* 1837. By the Rev. G. R. Gleig, M.A. Advertisement, pp. 4-8.

On *Prussia* Mr. Gleig's remarks are very full. Alas! they are too much in unison with his prefatory and more general observations in the first extract. I select them from different parts of his first volume :—

"'And your clergy (continued I)—are they without weight enough to make their example felt, even where their precept may fail in securing attention?'

"'Our clergy (replied he, with a smile)—why, yes, they are very excellent people in their way

his first publication as Christian Advocate of Cambridge University—"Observations on the attempted application of Pantheistic Principles to the Theory and Historic Criticism of the Gospel."

—very good men, without doubt; but really no human being pays the slightest regard either to what they say or what they do.'

"'Well, but the Gospel, on which your religion professes to be founded, is it quite held at nought among you?'

"My answer was another smile, of which I could not, without real pain, stop to analyze the import. He immediately added, however, as if conscious that he was treading upon delicate ground, 'The Gospels are by no means slightly estimated among us. We all admit that the code of morals taught in them is perfect; but—but—we don't profess to be guided by it.'

"If I had held this conversation with a very young or a very ignorant person—if a mere man of pleasure or (and the expression may perhaps carry more weight with it) a mere man of the world had so spoken to me—nay, if my own personal observations had not confirmed his statements, to an extent that was very painful, I should have been slow to give them credit, even at the moment, and still more slow to repeat them now. As it was, I could only lament the existence of a state of things so melancholy, and look round for causes which might account for it. The result of these enquiries I now proceed to lay before my reader; praying that, before my views be condemned, they may be judged with candour; and assuring him, that as they have not been taken up either lightly or in a spirit of prejudice, so am I quite ready to lay them down again whenever I shall have been convinced that they are founded in error."—*Gleig's Germany, &c.*, vol. i., p. 100.

"How, indeed, can a Government pretend to have the smallest regard for truth (and truth and religion are one and the same thing) which equally countenances the Protestant Episcopalian, the Presbyterian, the Papist, the Independent, the follower of the Greek Church, the Jew, and the Mahometan? It is quite clear that if these opposing parties have any one principle in common, it must be that they all inculcate known fables as truths; for their differences in other respects are so many and so great that they cannot equally deserve the countenance of any rational being. How, then, is the Government, which treats all as equally entitled to its respect, to escape the charge of utter indifference on the subject of religion? And be it observed that I am not pretending to decide which shall, and shall not, be treated as the true religion. My reasoning goes no further than this—that some one sect will, by a wise Government, be selected; that in the spirit of the creed taught by that sect will all its public arrangements, which affect the religion of the people, be guided. For religion in the abstract is a nonentity; and the religion of the Bible, as it is called, is nothing else than religion in the abstract. Men must be trained in infancy to worship God after some set forms, and to read the Scriptures according to some established system; otherwise it is much to be feared that they will soon cease to worship at all, and that the word of God will become valueless in their eyes. Let me apply this reasoning to the moral and religious condition of Prussia. In Prussia the clergy are universally poor. The living of Spandau, one of the richest in the kingdom, brings in an annual revenue of only two hundred Frederic d'ors, or one hundred and fifty or sixty pounds of our money. In the country places such is the depressed state of the clergy, that they are obliged, in many instances, to eke out their slender incomes by working in the fields like day labourers. Again, though the state religion of Prussia be Protestant (for the distinctions between Lutheran and Calvinist are now forgotten), such is the liberality of the Government, that in parishes where the majority of the inhabitants profess the Romish faith, a Romish priest draws the stipend, and occupies both the church and the glebe-house. Here, then, we have the two great evils already referred to—a clergy universally pauperized, and a State religion not fairly countenanced by the State. What is the consequence?"—*Ibid.*, pp. 109-111.

"I soon found, on pushing my enquiries further, that the relation between pastor and flock is, in Prussia, a very different affair from what it is among us. Nobody ever thought of applying to the pastor of ——, in case of difficulty, for advice. No sick person besought him to visit him or her in sickness. The poor found him not their advocate, nor expected so to find him. The bower-man sent him no little presents, eggs, or poultry, or fruit, in token of attachment. With the great proprietors, one of whom had a schloss in the parish, he held no intercourse; indeed he was, except in his own family, entirely companionless. Again, it was not his wont, nor the custom of his brethren, except on stated occasions, to catechize the young, or to exhort the aged. He lived, in short, a life of mere routine, and had no inclination to step beyond the circle. How is it possible that a man so circumstanced can have the slightest power to mould the opinions, or lay down rules for the conduct, of those around him? The errors, then, with which the Prussian Government seems to be chargeable are these: first, that it is not, in the proper acceptation of the term, in alliance with any particular church or creed whatever; and next, that it has not provided for the ministers of religion such a maintenance as the nature of their office requires. For it is beside the question to argue, that if the clergy be poor, they are at least on a level, in that respect, with the members of other professions. It can be no object to the Government whether the physician and apothecary shall have influence over the minds of his patients or not, or the lawyer be able to bend them to any given purpose. If the Government have a wish in reference to these gentlemen at all, it probably is, that they shall possess neither the inclination nor the will to sway the moral opinions of the people. But with the clergy the case is different. If they be incapable of accomplishing this end, they are clearly inadequate to perform one of the great purposes for which the State undertakes to maintain them. And I need scarcely add, that men are nowhere so humble-minded as to listen with deference, on the most important of all subjects, to the precepts of those whose condition renders all approach to general companionship impossible. Such, however, is precisely the state of things in Prussia; which is the more to be lamented, that the Government piques itself on the efforts which it makes to discover talent in other walks of life, and to foster and reward it. It is in the Church only that no prizes are bestowed, and that no pains are taken to ensure for the work of the ministry at least a fair share of the shining and influential genius which everywhere abounds in the community.

" I come now to another class of defects, for the existence and continued operation of which the Church, considered as a spiritual body, is entirely responsible. I allude to the absence of all discipline, all controlling power, over the religious opinions of the clergy, such as shall ensure a uniformity of doctrine in the public teaching of those to whom the people are to look for instruction in righteousness. I am not, indeed, ignorant that the doctrines set forth in the Confession of Augsburg are those to which the Lutheran Church professes to adhere. Neither have I forgotten that, for some time after the Reformation, subscription to that document, as well as to Melancthon's 'Apology,' and the rest of the symbolical books, was required of all candidates for holy orders; while of the labours of the old German divines, distinguished alike by their erudition and their piety, I am not willing to speak, except in terms of profound respect. But, besides that the symbolical books were, from the outset, at once too voluminous and too controversial to be rightly used as a confession of faith, the practice of subscribing to them arbitrarily was soon laid aside, and in its room a habit was adopted, which, in point of fact, rendered the act of subscription nugatory. As soon as men were permitted to declare their acceptance of these books only 'so far as they agreed with Scripture,' the utility of the books themselves, as a test of orthodoxy, ceased to exist; for such qualification clearly left each minister free to believe and to teach whatever his own fancy might dictate. With respect, again, to the Reformed Church, as the other great branch of Protestantism came to be called, it is extremely doubtful whether any test of orthodoxy was in it at any period applied; but it is certain that for a long while back nothing more has been required of him who offers himself for ordination than a promise that he will teach the people according to the Scriptures of God.

"Again, though there have been from the outset, in most of the Reformed Churches, forms appointed for public prayer and the administration of the sacraments it has never been the custom to require from the ministers a rigid attention to those forms. Some used them—others did not; and hence, even in the offering up of their devotions, the people were liable to be guided right or wrong, according to the humours or peculiar views of the pastor. Now, where there is neither a confession of faith, sanctioned by competent authority, nor a liturgy according to the spirit of which the worship of the people shall be directed, there is clearly no power anywhere of determining what shall, and what shall not, be the doctrine of the Church.

Bishops, or superintendents, or synods, or ecclesiastical courts, may be competent to restrain or to punish immoral practices in the clergy; but not having any acknowledged standard, according to which opinions may be tried, how can they interfere with men's doctrine? And if, in doctrine, a Church fall away from the simplicity of the Gospel, what reason have we to be surprised if the moral principle become likewise vitiated? I have ventured to assert that Prussia is not a religious and a moral country. Let me remind the reader of certain truths which bear upon the points now under consideration, and he will probably agree with me in thinking that a different result was not to be expected.

"Whoever will take the trouble to investigate the history of Protestantism in Germany, throughout the last eighty or ninety years, will find that the spectacle presented by it to the eye of the Christian is exceedingly sad. Throughout that extended period a large proportion of the Reformed divines have not only rejected for themselves all belief in the divine origin of Christianity, but have laboured, with a zeal worthy of a better cause, to instil their own pernicious opinions into the minds of others. From the chairs of the theological professorships in the Universities, of which, at one time, they had monopolized the possession, as well as in the pages of all the most influential literary and religious journals, which were chiefly under their control, a body of Rationalists, as they called themselves, ceased not to condemn and hold up to ridicule all who professed their belief in particular inspirations; nay, the very pulpits became, in their hands, and in those of their disciples, fountains from which came forth continually the waters which canker where they flow. Moreover, the amount of learning which they brought to aid them in this unholy task was undeniably as great, as the skill which they displayed in adapting their arguments to the tastes and comprehensions of the different classes in society was remarkable. No wonder that the consequences should have been a speculative infidelity everywhere, producing its necessary result—a ruinous relaxation in all the moral restraints and obligations of social life."—*Ibid.*, pp. 115-121.

"To the principle introduced into historical criticism by Heyne, and the theory set up in reference to the human intellect by Kant, the low ebb to which religious feeling sank in Protestant Germany is in a great measure to be attributed. The former, weary of the verbal trifling of his predecessors, struck into a different path, and from the wildest flights of the classical poets brought forth statements illustrative of the progress of civilization from age to age, and the institutions and manners of other times. The latter, dissatisfied with the views both of Leibnitz and Malebranche, and utterly contemning those of Berkeley, assumed as his maxim, that the human mind is infallible; in other words, that no postulate in metaphysics ought to be regarded as true, of which the fitness is not demonstrable to our reasoning faculties. There was great boldness, as well as some novelty, in the views both of the scholar and the philosopher; and the boldness or novelty in dealing with such matters is sure to attract attention in Germany. A fresh impulse seemed to be given to the learning of the age. What Heyne had done in reference to the mythology of the Greek poets, his imitators hastened to do in elucidation of the treatises which compose the Old and New Testaments; while Kant's principle was fearlessly applied to the doctrines deduced from these treatises. Semler, Teller, Steinbart, and Eberhard, demonstrated, to the satisfaction of all the Neologists of the day, that Moses and Homer were alike deserving of credit; that the Hebrew judges ought to take rank with the Greek heroes; that Isaiah and Joel, and the rest of the Prophets, were the political Reformers of their respective ages; and that Jesus Christ was but the Socrates of Judea. It is melancholy to recollect with what thunders of applause the ravings of these and other sciolists were greeted, and how rapid was the progress which their opinions made, especially among the young and the aspiring, both of the clergy and the laity.

"There was no authority in any of the Protestant Churches of Germany to protest against these heresies; far less to expel from her communion the men who taught them. Individual champions were never, indeed, wanting to the truth; for the treatises of Storr and his friends, of Flatt, and Suskind, and others, remain as lasting monuments of their own powers, and of the good sense of those by whom they were read and approved: but the stream of popularity ran against them, and it set in with greatest violence in the situations where, of all others, it was sure to bring the most mischievous results in its train. The remuneration bestowed upon the professors at the German Universities is so inadequate, that there is imposed upon them the necessity of giving what are called private lectures. For these the students pay; and such became, by degrees, the craving after novelty, that no man, who was not known to hold ancient prejudices in contempt, could hope to gather a moderately numerous class about him. Moreover, the young men dismissed from College, and, as yet, unprovided for in the Church, usually find employment in Germany as tutors in private families, or assistants in schools. In these situations they indulged freely the tastes which they had acquired at the University; and, last of all, carried with them to their respective parishes, not only the habits of mere students, but a fatal exemption, in the prosecution of their enquiries, from everything like an established principle of faith.

"I do not deny that the description which has just been given is more applicable, perhaps, to what the state of things in Protestant Germany was some years ago, than to what we find it now. The Rationalist school, among the clergy at least, is neither so large nor so much in the ascendant as it used to be, though it still can boast of a very considerable number of men eminent for their learning and their zeal. The influence of such names as Ammon, Schott, Bretschneider, and Wegschneider, is not to be lightly dealt with; and though the first of these may have, in some sort, abandoned his original views, it is not quite clear, judging from the tone of his later writings, that he ever adopted the truths of the Gospel in their simplicity. Meanwhile, a new school, that of the Mystics, is rising into note; so that, by and by, the Protestant Churches bid fair to be divided into the absolute worshippers of reason on the one hand, and mere enthusiasts on the other. I do not mean, under this head, to include Dr. Hengstenberg, of Berlin, to whose labours the cause of truth is so much indebted, Dr. Tholuck, of Halle, or Dr. Neander, the admirable author of ' The History of Paganism.' These, with many more, have stood forth nobly in the forefront of the battle; but, somehow or another, their writings carry with them much less of weight than those which go to either of the opposite extremes—enthusiasm or infidelity. It is something, however, to be able to say that revelation, in its purity and simplicity, has its champions in Protestant Germany;

and recent proceedings on the part of the Prussian Government show that there is, at least, no disposition among those in power to give further countenance to anything else. I do not find that the Protestant Church has, as yet, drawn up its confession of faith, or assumed the right, which seems inherent in all Churches, of determining what doctrines its ministers shall, and what they shall not, teach; ut with a liturgy the king has supplied it. In Prussia there is now a Book of Common Prayer, which Lutherans, and Calvinists, and even French Protestants, use in common; so that from the hazard of being misled, at least in the offering up of their devotions, the people are happily delivered."—*Ibid.*, pp. 125-130.

On his visit to Dresden the author makes similar observations on the Church of Saxony. They are necessarily not so much in detail, for the reason assigned in the first sentence of the following paragraph :—

" The observations which I have hazarded in reference to the Lutheran Church of Prussia will apply very nearly to the state of the same

Church in Saxony, except in this—that the clergy have much more weight in the management of the national education here, than they have, or can ever expect to attain, in Prussia. In Dresden, as Berlin, there is a Minister of Public Instruction, who superintends the working of a machinery not dissimilar, in its main features, to that which operates in Prussia; but his council, instead of acting by sections, from the most important of which ecclesiastics are shut out, acts as one body, and is composed mainly of ecclesiastics. In like manner, the village schools come, at least in theory, much more under the immediate control of the pastor; and at the Universities, as well as in the gymnasia, ecclesiastical influence is paramount. Still the extreme poverty of the clergy, the humble station which they fill in society, the habits which of necessity they acquire, and their general ignorance, all render them, as guides of public feeling, and controllers of public principle, virtually inefficient. The Saxons are not, in any class, a religious people; and if, in some, they deserve to be accounted virtuous, the merit of their virtue is due, certainly not to the exertions of the clergy, but in part, perhaps, to constitutional coldness—

in part to the good example which is set them by the court."—*Ibid.*, p. 202.

The last extract which I shall make from Mr. Gleig's interesting work—and eminently useful for his views of the state of religion in the countries he visited—is his very just remark on the desecration of the Lord's-day in Saxony:—

"When we come to the region of morals, I should say, that, though higher than that of Prussia, the standard in Saxony is not very elevated. There is here the same lamentable deficiency of religious principle which we find all over Protestant Germany. People may or may not go to Church on a Sunday, and their children they send to school because the law requires it; but the practices which, more than all others, mark the degree of reverence in which men hold their religion, are here unknown. I never heard of a family in which prayers were daily said, nor knew an instance of a child being trained by its parent to the habit of private devotion; and as to the mode of observing the Lord's-day, I confess that I do not see on what grounds a Christian can defend it. Not content with holding their little revels in the evening before the inn, or amid the public gardens, they seem to regard the prosecution of their ordinary employments as no breach of the divine will. I have repeatedly seen both men and women hoeing in the fields, and working in the shoe-shop, just as busily on a Sunday as on any other day in the week."—*Ibid.*, p. 234.

Note R, Page 59.

INFIDELITY OF SCOTCH METAPHYSICIANS: HUME, BOLINGBROKE, AND GIBBON; AND THE METAPHYSICAL TENDENCY OF CALVIN'S PECULIAR DOCTRINES.

I have heard with surprise and regret that the passage referred to in the text has been supposed to contain a national reflection. Such a feeling and such a purpose, could it be seriously suspected of me, I disclaim. It were altogether unworthy in itself; it were especially indecorous in so sacred a place, and on so solemn an occasion; and it were eminently unbecoming, personally and professionally, a preacher of the Gospel.

But TRUTH must be always avowed when occasion calls for the avowal. The truth declared in the text unhappily accords but too strictly with the subject of the discourse. The metaphysicians of Scotland, and her literary men, about the conclusion of the last century and the beginning of the present, undoubtedly were foremost in the ranks of infidelity. Of the metaphysicians towards the conclusion of the last century, one name—in himself a host of that unhappy association—David Hume, the philosopher and historian, will at once rise to the reader's memory. He had, indeed, lived in France, and he may be said to represent that apostate faction, the French Encyclopædists, and the arch-apostate Voltaire, who laid the embers which, when inflamed, produced the French Revolution, but which were not blown into flame until some years after the death of Hume. But we know not what temper of mind may be engendered by the subtil law of the association of ideas; and metaphysical subtilty is inseparable from Calvinistic countries. Scepticism, as well as faith, is undoubtedly the fruit of the tree of knowledge of good and evil. Happily, the philosophical writings of Hume are now not widely read. But I have known in my own time disciples of this sceptical metaphysician. The only copy I have read of his Essays, and which I now possess, was presented to me by a person at least twenty-five years since, whose mind, I fear, had been deeply infected with the "science falsely so called" of pyrrhonism. Yet I confess that his Essay on Miracles, the *chef-d'œuvre* of his unholy works, ever appeared to me a very shallow performance.

Hume was preceded and followed by Englishmen of the infidel philosophical school. The writings of Lord Bolingbroke, which were cut into shreds by the mighty hand of Warburton, were of a character peculiar to himself personally, and to the age generally in Europe, rather than characteristic of the English, or of any other nation. He was, as he has been truly styled by Archbishop Magee, in a work already cited and referred to in this Appendix,* properly a "SOPHIST," and a very superficial member of that superficial class.

Hume had one *disciple* in England; for such I have ever regarded the historian of the "Decline and Fall of the Roman Empire." Gibbon, in his letters, always speaks with admiration of Hume; and somewhere he calls him, with complacency, "the fattest swine of the Epicurean sty." The light of Gibbon's fame arose with the setting sun of Hume's earthly existence, which went down with the utterance of the impious levities detailed by his friend

* See Ante, Note N. The reader may consult Magee on the Atonement, vol. ii., pp. 255-257, for an able exposition of these two infidels, Bolingbroke and Hume.

Adam Smith, which still disgrace the editions of his History of England. In a letter of Mr. Wallace to Mr. Strahan, concerning the death of Hume, inserted among Gibbon's correspondence, is the following passage:—" It has been remarked, that the same day on which Lucretius died, gave birth to Virgil; and amidst their late severe loss, philosophy and literature will probably find themselves not wholly disconsolate, on reflecting that the same year in which they were deprived of Hume, Gibbon arose."*

I am tempted to say something more of Gibbon, though it be not exactly the subject of the text, but it is in alliance with it. Gibbon's history, as narrated by himself in his own most interesting memoirs, accounts for the *unsettling* of his mind; but his *settling* on infidelity in the form it took in his mind seems to have been very much influenced by his brother historian,

---

* Gibbon's Miscellaneous Works, vol. ii., p. 175, 8vo. edition.

the Scotch philosopher, David Hume. He glories in the designation of a philosopher. He wrote, indeed, no philosophical essays against Christianity; but he insinuated objections by the falsification of history. His too well known fifteenth and sixteenth chapters are the most elaborate special pleading. They, perhaps, cost him more labour than some volumes of his history, being condensed from an octavo volume, with which fact he acquaints us in his Memoirs. But his artful elevation of the characters of the apostate Julian and the impostor Mahomet, and the depression of the Divine Founder of Christianity, are his greatest achievements in his evil design. The poison is thus insinuated into the whole body of his history. His great auxiliary throughout was grave ridicule, as too accurately described by the noble and sceptical author of " Childe Harold :"—

"He sapped a solemn creed with solemn sneer,
　The lord of irony."

Among all the literary men who corresponded with Gibbon, Mr. Whitaker, the learned antiquary—the author of "The History of Manchester," and a variety of other works, of which "The History of Arianism" is one—is the only person who broadly and openly rebuked him for his attacks upon Christianity. He thus boldly writes, in a letter* thanking him for his first volume :†—

"You never speak feebly except when you come on British ground, and never weakly except when you attack Christianity. In the former case, you seem to me to want information; and in the latter, you plainly want the common candour of a citizen of the world for the religious system of your country. Pardon me, sir, but much as I admire your abilities, greatly as I respect your friendship, I cannot bear without indignation your sarcastic slyness upon Christianity, and cannot see without pity your determined hostility to the Gospel."

* Dated April 21, 1776. Miscellaneous Works, vol. ii., p. 146. 8vo. edition.
† In 4to., two of the 8vo. ones.

Again, in a second letter,* alluding to the first, he says :—

"You also received my animadversions upon your history with candour. I was particularly pointed, I believe, in what I said concerning the religious part of it. I wrote from my feelings at the time; and was, perhaps, the less inclined to suppress those feelings from friendliness, because I had two favours to beg of you. I hope I shall ever be attached, with every power of my judgment and my affection, to that glorious system of truth which is the vital principle of happiness to my soul in time and in eternity. And in this I act not from any 'restraints of profession:' I should despise myself if I did. I act from the fullest conviction of a mind that has been a good deal exercised in enquiries into truth, and that has shown, I fancy, a strong spirit of rational scepticism, in rejecting and refuting a variety of opinions which have passed current for ages in our national histories."

He reverts to the subject at the conclusion of the same letter in a like bold and

* May 11, 1776. Miscellaneous Works, vol. ii., pp. 149-151.

uncompromising style. He calls his religious scepticism and scorn " the great blot of his work."

"You have there (he continues) exhibited Deism in a new shape, and in one that is more likely to affect the uninstructed millions, than the reasoning form which she has usually worn. You seem to me like another Tacitus, revived with all his animosity against Christianity, his strong philosophical spirit of sentiment, and more than his superiority to the absurdities of heathenism; and you will have the dishonour (pardon me, sir) of being ranked by the folly of scepticism, that is working so powerfully at present, among the most distinguished Deists of the age. I have long suspected the tendency of your opinions. I once took the liberty of hinting my suspicions. But I did not think the poison had spread so universally through your frame. And I can only deplore the misfortune, and a very great one I consider it, to the highest and dearest interests of man among all your readers."

These remarks are spirited, noble, and severe. This is the duty of every avowed champion of the truth. These letters were not inserted in the first edition, in quarto, of the historian's miscellaneous works; and the noble editor, Lord Sheffield, the bosom friend of Gibbon, and his executor, but lamely apologizes for their omission. " If the letters of Mr. Whitaker (he states in a note) *had been perused previously to the publication of the former edition*, this manly and spirited declaration in favour of the principles of the Established Church, against the perversion of those opinions which constitute the greatest comfort and consolation of the Christian world, would not have been then withheld from the public." I confess, to me it does seem strange that *such* letters should have been withheld. No answer appears to these letters. Gibbon knew the weakness and the strength of his enemies: he demolishes Davis and such antagonists; while he flatters Watson, and is silent to the spirited Whitaker.

But if we compare the historian of Manchester with the rest of the correspondents of the historian of " The Decline and

Fall," the result will be, that there is a melancholy want of right feeling and principle in almost all. The only exception is Priestley, who, heretic as himself was, boldly and uncompromisingly charges Gibbon with his infidelity.

Mr. Gibbon, as appears from his Miscellaneous Works, had two correspondents who have left the record to posterity of a much more courtly, or, to speak plainly, a much less straightforward and faithful spirit than the manly and healthy tone of Mr. Whitaker, so worthy of a clergyman, and a presbyter of the Church of England. These are Bishop Watson, already mentioned, and the historian, Dr. Robertson, Principal of the University of Edinburgh, and a leading minister of the Presbyterian Establishment of Scotland. A bishop of the Church of England, and a doctor of divinity of the Scotch Kirk, OUGHT, we might not uncharitably suppose, to have dealt somewhat more plainly and strongly with a scoffing infidel such as Gibbon, however personally they esteemed him, and, as a writer, admired him; seeing that BOTH were equally bound " earnestly to contend for the faith which was once delivered to the saints." But let us see.

In a letter of Gibbon to his friend Mr. Holroyd, afterwards Lord Sheffield, in 1776, he thus writes:—" An anonymous pamphlet and Dr. Watson out against me —(in my opinion) the former feeble and very illiberal; *the latter uncommonly genteel.*"* I happen not to have Bishop Watson's work by me; but the " uncommonly genteel" passage is that, I apprehend, which is embodied in Gibbon's " Vindication" of his proscribed fifteenth and sixteenth chapters against Mr. Davis, who, instead of attacking him boldly upon his infidelity, questions the accuracy of his scholarship—and is overthrown. In this pamphlet occurs this remarkable passage respecting Dr. Watson:—†

---

* Gibbon's Miscellaneous Works, vol. ii., p. 176.
† Gibbon's Miscellaneous Works, vol. iv., p. 597.

"When Dr. Watson gave to the public his 'Apology for Christianity,' in a series of letters, he addressed them to the author of the 'Decline and Fall of the Roman Empire,' with a just confidence that he had considered this important object in a manner not unworthy of his antagonist or of himself. *Dr. Watson's mode of thinking bears a liberal and a philosophic cast; his thoughts are expressed with spirit, and that spirit is always tempered by politeness and moderation.* Such is the man whom I should be happy to call my friend, and whom I should not blush to call my antagonist. But the same motives which might tempt me to accept, or even to solicit, a private and amicable conference, dissuaded me from entering into a public controversy with a writer of so respectable a character; and I embraced the earliest opportunity of expressing to Dr. Watson himself how sincerely I agreed with him in thinking, '*that as the world is now of the opinion of us both upon the subject in question, it may be perhaps as proper for us both to leave it in this state possessed.*'"*

Now the wiliness and the cowardice of

* Watson's " Apology for Christianity," p. 200.

the historian are obvious throughout this transaction. He beats down such weak antagonists as Davis and others, who merely question his scholarship, with the most unmitigated sarcasm, and the most sovereign contempt. But Dr. Watson, who attacks his infidel opinions, he conciliates and flatters; and though he most grossly attacks Christianity in its most vital part, and sends out his falsification of Ecclesiastical History to the whole world, he would settle the difference with the only writer who was a worthy opponent in strength, by "*a private and amicable conference,*" instead of "a *pubic controversy.*" If any controversy should be public and uncompromising, it surely should be with a man who, before all the world, endeavours to loosen the ties of the love of man for his God and Redeemer, by undermining the very foundations of truth.

And I grieve that a prelate of our venerable Church should have accepted such an unhallowed compromise. In reply to a letter, or rather a note or card, of Gibbon, printed in the correspondence of the historian, in which he says they both may employ their time much more usefully, as well as agreeably, than they could possibly do by exhibiting a single combat in the amphitheatre of controversy, but adds that "he still reserves to himself the privilege of inserting in a future edition some occasional remarks and explanations of his meaning;" in reply to this, Dr. Watson allows him the privilege he claims of repeating his offence by *further* "remarks and explanations," in these words:—" It would be very extraordinary if Mr. Gibbon did not feel a parent's partiality for an offspring which has justly excited the admiration of all who have seen it; and Dr. Watson would be the last person in the world to wish him to suppress any explanation which might tend to exalt its merits."*

* Gibbon's Miscellaneous Works, vol. ii., p. 181.

So did the wily Greek of old introduce the perilous machine of armed men into the heart of the Trojan city; and a Christian bishop should have suspected the gifts of the modern Greek. While truth compels us to state such things, let us take warning, and not make weak concessions to the enemies of the faith, in whatever form they may appear.*

Does the Presbyterian divine and the brother historian appear in fairer colours in this correspondence? The record preserved in Gibbon's miscellaneous papers, published after his death, equally condemns Dr. Robertson of deserting his post at the citadel of the faith, and going over to the enemy. In a letter to Mr. Strahan, dated Edinburgh College,† March 15,

---

* There is another letter of Dr. Watson's to Gibbon (p. 227 of the same volume), in which he "begs the historian's pardon for the declaration of his belief." But for this the letter is admirable; but this spoils all.

† A place which should have reminded the Principal that he was the guardian of youth, as well as a minister of the Gospel.

1776, he thus expresses himself like one of *the trade*:—" I have not yet read the two last chapters, but am sorry, from what I have heard of them, that he has taken such a tone in them as will give great offence, and *hurt the sale of the book*.* It *did* " give great offence;" but as it did *not* " hurt the sale of the book," the friendly Principal and brother historian seems to have become so far reconciled to the infidel and his writings, as never to advert to the subject in his correspondence with Gibbon himself, who tells him that " the most ambitious wish he entertained was to obtain the approbation of Dr. Robertson and Mr. Hume—two names which friendship united, and which posterity will never separate."†

Now this is natural on the part of Gibbon, a young man, who had just published his first (but most offensive) volume. But

---

* Gibbon's Miscellaneous Works, vol. ii., p. 160.
† Gibbon's Miscellaneous Works, vol. ii., p. 202.

Dr. Robertson, a minister of religion, has, perhaps, done more injury to the cause of Christianity than can be known until the Great Day, by being handed down to posterity as the intimate friend of Hume and Gibbon, the most inveterate enemies of our holy faith that the world has seen, except, perhaps, their compeer and contemporary, Voltaire, and Julian the apostate. In the answer to this letter of Gibbon, his friendship is accepted most unconditionally. Of his friendship with Hume, the Doctor says —"I am much pleased with your mentioning my friendship with Mr. Hume; I have always considered that as one of the most fortunate and honourable circumstances of my life." He adds—" In the intercourse between Mr. Hume and me, we always found *something to blame* as well as *something to commend.** I had received frequently very valuable criticism, &c." The blame and commendation, therefore, were

* So printed in the letter, *Ibid.*, p. 204.

always *literary!* Literature and friendship are indeed good things, the delight and the solace of our lives; but surely truth and religion are better than the finest books in the world without them. Nor can I deem that man my friend who is an open enemy of his God and Redeemer —"Amicus Plato, amicus homo, sed major amica VERITAS."

In another letter, on the controversy with Davis, Dr. Robertson says—"Though I have watched you with some attention, I have not observed any expression which I should, on your account, wish to be altered."* The pamphlet is an able one; but why such complaisance? The subject, a matter of criticism, did not admit of anything very offensive. But the tone

---

* Gibbon's Miscellaneous Works, vol. ii., p. 229. The whole letter is in the same complimentary strain. In another letter (p. 249 of the same volume), he compliments Gibbon most extravagantly on his "Reign of Julian"—truly, one of the most covert and malignant attacks on the Christian faith which even Gibbon has put forth.

of the greater part of it jars on the ear of faith; and particular passages, such as those on Eusebius, in my humble judgment, *might* have been "altered" and amended.

There are few works on my own shelves, and in the language, which I have perused more attentively, and often with the greatest delight, than the miscellaneous works of this celebrated historian. They are abundantly more interesting than his great work. They are full of variety, and combine biography with the spirit and love of literature, rarely met with even in the lives of literary men. The style of his memoirs and familiar letters is unstilted and natural. "His Journals to a Student are above all price." Passages, moreover, of genuine beauty and eloquence, in the Memoirs particularly, linger in the memory, from the first reading of them, during all our after years. Such is his description of his first entrance into the "*eternal* *city;*"* his first conception of his laborious work, as he sat musing amidst the ruins of the capital, while the barefooted friars were singing vespers in the Temple of Jupiter;† and, above all, his beautiful account of his emotions on his ‡ "final deliverance" of his history of the "Decline and Fall," which, with all its faults, is one of the most delightful works in any language.

But feeling and allowing all this, the pleasure to a reflecting Christian is not only not unmixed, but it is alloyed with the substance of extreme pain. Wandering

---

* "My temper is not very susceptible of enthusiasm, and the enthusiasm which I do not feel I have ever scorned to affect. But, at the distance of twenty five years, I can neither forget nor express the strong emotions which agitated my mind as I first approached and entered the *eternal city*. After a sleepless night, I trod, with a lofty step, the ruins of the forum; each memorable spot where Romulus *stood*, or Tully spoke, or Cæsar fell, was at once present to my eye; and several days of intoxication were lost or enjoyed before I could descend to a cool and minute investigation."—*Miscellaneous Works*, vol. i., p. 194.

† *Ibid.*, p. 198. ‡ *Ibid.*, p. 255.

amid his works is like wandering amid the ruins of the "eternal city." Instead of being ETERNAL, it is in ruin. Thus is the mind, so richly gifted, without the hope of everlasting life. Not only DEISM, but ATHEISM, is unveiled in his miscellaneous and posthumous works. Not only does he deny the moral providence of God, but he seems to exclude God from the universe; all is nature and chance.

Why Robertson was so carefully forbearing with Gibbon is not easy to be discovered or conjectured. He has been accused of partaking the scepticism of his two great compeers and contemporaries. From this imputation he has been honourably rescued by a countryman of his own, and of a different communion—a bishop of the Scotch Episcopal Church,* who superintended an edition of his works, and prefixed a Life, and a sermon on "the situation of the world at the time of Christ's

* Bishop Glegi's Edit., Edin., 1818.

appearance, &c., preached before the Society in Scotland for Propagating Christian Knowledge, January 6, 1755." The Right Reverend Editor says of it, that it "is the only specimen of Dr. Robertson's pulpit eloquence which has come down to us, and is in all respects worthy of its author."

In his fifteenth and sixteenth chapters, the most elaborate pieces of sophistry perhaps ever composed, Gibbon follows the track of Mosheim, a Presbyterian, respecting the government of the Church in the first three centuries. This may have had some influence in making the whole less offensive to Presbyterians, and Dissenters generally.

But the main source of that culpable tolerance of Gibbon's opinions, published in his work, as well as of the grossness of many passages and numerous notes, was what, though used with a far different application, may be emphatically termed a

'FATAL FACILITY"—a want of that fixed principle and moral courage, to utter unpleasant and offensive truths, so rare among frail and corrupt men.*

I have dwelt so much on Gibbon because I could not separate him from the Scottish school of infidelity, of which he has always appeared to me to be a pupil; and because his personal history, and that

---

* That Gibbon's deep-rooted infidelity, so far as the mind of man can perceive, terminated only with his life, we may collect from the following interesting passage of Forster's " Life of Bishop Jebb :"—" Sunday, May 12, 1833. This morning, I pointed out to the bishop a melancholy passage, in the first volume of Dr. Currie's memoirs, respecting EDWARD GIBBON, in which the historian is described as expressing to Mrs. Holroyd, a few days before death, the little or no hope he had of a future life, and his contentment with annihilation!" My friend's reply was —" No one can say what may have taken place in his mind, even in the last day or two. I was once drowned (alluding to his all but fatal accident, at Rosstrevor, more than five and thirty years before), and I know, by experience, how much thought may be crowded into a single moment." On my enquiring whether he distinctly recollected the sensations he experienced while under water, he replied— " There was a great stunning, but I well recollect that a vast train of thought came, on the moment, into my mind."—*Forster's Life of Bishop Jebb*, pp. 277, 278. Second edition. London. 1837.

of his friends, hold out a salutary warning to clergy, and Churchmen, lay or clerical, always to speak the truth on great subjects, such as those of our holy religion, when occasion calls for it, without fear, favour, or affection to any individual.

I need but mention the authors and editors of the "Edinburgh Review," at the beginning of the present century, as the abettors of principles and doctrines utterly subversive of all religious truth and civil subordination. This was, at first, purely a Scotch work.

It only remains that I offer a very few remarks on the metaphysical tendency of Calvin's peculiar doctrines, as it affects the character of the people. How this turn of mind and process of thought lead to greater and deeper evils, in respect of DOCTRINE, will be shown in a subsequent note.

Calvin's doctrine of Predestination* has

---

* "Calvinistic Predestination is not in the Bible."
—*Alex. Knox.*

ESTABLISHED, rather than introduced, not only an entirely new species of doctrine, but it has created a new mode of thought, and a new set of religious feelings, by the abstruse and metaphysical reasoning it has fastened on biblical criticism. The whole Bible is to be bent in the direction of the peculiar construction of a few chapters of St. Paul's Epistle to the Romans. Metaphysical refinements being constantly heard from the pulpit, the people have become insensibly imbued with a close-thinking, reasoning character of mind. The cool-headed Scotchman carries this character into the world, and his shrewdness avails him in temporal affairs. He moves in a narrow way, but strongly, like a narrow current of water. Sometimes, indeed, he reasons himself out of his faith: hence the scepticism both of Scotland and Geneva. But it appears to me that the Calvinistic creed has, in all countries where it has prevailed, moulded the national character.

Note S, Page 60.

INNOVATIONS OF CALVIN.

It may excite surprise, and perhaps displeasure in some, that I speak of the venerable Calvin as "the greatest innovator" of the Church, perhaps since the time of Arius. And yet it is but the language of most respectable authorities—learned and pious laymen, as well as more professional divines. Calvin was an innovator in Church discipline and government; he was an innovator in doctrine, and he was "the greatest innovator" in the sacrament of baptism.

That he was an innovator in the discipline and government of the Church, the discipline and Presbyterian government of all national establishments and sects formed upon his model are abundant evidence. That he was an innovator in doctrine—and that doctrine the holy and ever blessed Trinity—I shall proceed to show.

The late Alexander Knox, truly styled a "Christian philosopher," in that beautiful work, the "Thirty Years' Correspondence with Bishop Jebb,"* in one of his Letters (57) writes thus, touching the innovating spirit of the Genevan Reformer:—

"I am glad you have taken that disporting walk through the paths of the ancients. Your own idea, founded on the article in the Athanasian Creed, I conceive very just; and I suppose a particular attention to our Lord's manner of speaking respecting Himself would add still more and more strength to it—His language being, I imagine, always θεανθρωποπρεπης, except

---

* The following remarks of the late Mrs. Hemans ("Life of Henry F. Chorley," vol. ii., p. 329) will not be read with indifference:—"I can only tell you of several works which I have read with strong and varied interest. Amongst the chief of these has been the correspondence of Bishop Jebb with Mr. Knox, which presents, I think, the most beautiful picture ever developed of a noble Christian friendship, brightening on and into 'perfect day,' through an uninterrupted period of thirty years. Knox's part of the correspondence is extremely rich in original thought and the highest views of enlightened Christian philosophy. There is much elegance, pure religion, and refined intellectual taste in the bishop's letters also, but his mind is decidedly inferior both in fervour and power."

when He meant to conceal His real nature. If you have Nelson's* "Life of Bull," you will find the whole matter in debate largely expatiated on (sect lvii., &c.) in the account of the Fidei Nicænæ Defensio; and, what is curious, *Calvin appears to be the great antagonist of the ancient doctrine*—WHAT A UNIVERSAL INNOVATOR THAT MAN WAS! And yet it seems that his zeal against the subordination did not imply equal zeal for

* The reader is referred to an excellent article of the *British Critic* for January, 1838 (No. xlv., art. vi., p. 113), for a severe but just exposition of the authors of " Two Memorials, addressed to the General Meeting of the Society for Promoting Christian Knowledge, and the alleged corrupt character of some of its publications" (London, 1837). These memorials were presented by five Essex ministers, whose names are given. Certain works, which we have always regarded, from father to son, as most pious, primitive, and practical books, and perfectly orthodox—such as " Nelson's Festivals" and " The Whole Duty of Man" — are by these memorialists charged with Popery, and wished to be expunged from the Society's list. If this party in the Church think to stem the tide of Popery by taking away from the people our most pious and practical works of truly orthodox men, such as Nelson and the author of " The Whole Duty of Man," they will find to their cost that they are doing the work of the enemy. It is by the old and orthodox clergy, and by publications such as those of the seventeenth century, that Popery will be only and effectually opposed. Hence the deep hatred of the Romish Church to the pure Catholic Church of England and her followers.

sameness of nature. Thus, you see, the apparently highest ground is not always the safest. But how natural was it in Calvin to take the ground that excluded from his faith what he so strongly rejected in practice, personally no less than ecclesiastically. In fact, *subordination* was not a term in John Calvin's vocabulary. But the worst of it was, that, by not allowing such an order in the Divine Essence as would safely explain certain texts which seem to exclude strict co-ordinateness, he created a necessity for himself and his followers to explain them, when accidentally occurring, in a manner not strictly consistent with the co-essentiality; *all which, however, evinces more and more that Calvinism, altogether, is a temporary scaffolding which has so little firm work in it, as to need time, and its own weight only, at length to bring it down."—Thirty Years' Correspondence*, vol. i., p. 416. Second edition.

The passage from Nelson's "Life of Bishop Bull" is here subjoined, that the entire subject may be seen at once:—

" Now concerning the subordination of the

Son, as to his original from the Father, Mr. Bull hath laid down and proved these three following theses, viz.:—1. *'That decree of the Nicene Council, by which it is declared that the Son of God is God of God [Θεος εκ Θεου], is generally approved of by the Catholic doctors, both by them that lived before and them that lived after that Council; for they all with one consent have taught, that the divine nature and perfections do agree to the Father and Son, not collaterally or co-ordinately, but subordinately—that is, that the Son hath indeed the same divine nature in common with the Father, but hath it communicated from the Father, so as the Father alone hath that divine nature from Himself, or from no other besides, but the Son from the Father; and consequently, that the Father is the fountain, original, and principle of the divinity which is in the Son. 2. † The Catholic writers, both they that were before and they that were after the Council of Nice, have unanimously declared God the Father to be greater than the Son, even according to His divinity: yet this is not by nature indeed, or by any essential perfection which is

---

* Sect. iv., cap. 1. † Cap. 11.

in the Father, and is wanting in the Son; but only by fatherhood, or His being the author and original; forasmuch as the Son is from the Father, not the Father from the Son. 3. The doctrine of the subordination of the Son to the Father, as to his origination and principiation, the ancients thought to be most useful, and even altogether necessary to be known and believed, that by this means the Godhead of the Son might be so asserted, as that the unity of God, nevertheless, and the divine monarchy, might still be preserved inviolate. Forasmuch as notwithstanding the name and nature are common to two, that is, to the Father and to the Son, yet because one is the principle of the other, from whom He is propagated, and that by internal, not external production, it thence followeth that God may rightly be said to be but one God. And the same ancients believed, moreover, that the very same reason did hold likewise as to the Godhead of the Holy Ghost.' This is the sum of his doctrine concerning the divine monarchy and subordination in the blessed Trinity, so as not to lessen either the consubstantiality or co-eternity of the Son and Spirit with the Father. For though he maintained that there are in the

Deity three really distinct hypostases or persons, he no less strenuously insisteth that there is and can be but one God; first, because there is but one fountain or principle of the Godhead, viz.: —The FATHER! who only is [Αυτοθεος] God of and from Himself, the SON and HOLY GHOST deriving from Him their divinity: and then because the SON and HOLY GHOST are so derived from the fountain of the divinity, as not to be separate or separable from it, but always to exist therein most intimately united.

"Under each of these three last theses there are some considerable observations made by our author, from the Catholic doctors of the Church, both before and after the rise of Arianism; without a thorough understanding of which, it will be impossible ever to settle this matter to satisfaction. In treating the first of them, he hath learnedly and solidly confuted the unreasonable and uncatholic notion of the moderns, which maketh the Son a self-dependent principle of divinity (and, by consequence, another God), by asserting and defending, that He might properly be called Αυτοθεος, as well as the Father is, and that He is truly God of Himself, and not God of God, as the Nicene fathers confess Him. This opinion was first of all started by Calvin* against the judgment of the Catholic Church to this very day, and even of the first Reformers, Luther and Melancthon, as Petavius and our author have sufficiently shown. It was afterwards dressed up and vindicated by Danæus,† and after him by several others of the Calvinistical school; whose main argument was this, that Christ must have been God of Himself, or also He could not be God at all; because the notion of God supposeth self-existence. This opinion was very much opposed, about the end of the sixteenth and the beginning of the seventeenth century, by Arminius, in an epistolary dissertation on this subject, to one Vytenbogard, in his declaration made before the States of Holland; in his apology against the one and thirty articles; and lastly, in a letter to the Prince Palatine's Envoyée to the States General. But the prejudices which many entertained against him were so violent, as none of his arguments could get to be heard by them, who were so bigotted to their master, and to his private opinions, as not to be able to bear anything

* Inst. Theol., lib. i., caps. 13, § 19.
† Isagy Chris., lib. i., caps. 23.

which might grate but never so little upon the esteem they had for him, and for theses, which were looked upon by them as so many Evangelical discoveries. This seems to be the true state of the matter; whence this controversy was still kept up by some of the more zealous antiremonstrants, notwithstanding the great weight of evidence brought for the old Catholic doctrine against them in this article.

"Some went so far as even to ridicule the Nicene Creed upon this account, and call the fathers who composed it a parcel of fanatics,* for styling therein Christ, *God of God, Light of Light*, &c.; and some ran also hence into Sabellian† explications of this mystery, even to the taking away of all distinctions of hypostases in the Godhead, as by our author hath been well observed. Bellarmin and Petavius have been too severe, however, upon Calvin for his mistake; but Possevin ‡ still more so, by whom it is named the heresy of the Anthotheans; and the founder of it, the new Tritheist. But there is none, after all, to be compared with a certain

* Vid. Defen. Fid. Nic., sect. iv., cap. 1, § 8.
† Ibid., § 7, 9, et Epist. i., Armin. ad 5 Vytenbog.
‡ Lib de Atheis Hær., cap. vi., p. 14, edit. Colog. 1586.

Austrian Jesuit,* the author of a book called 'Symbola Tria,' who hath been at the pains to collect several passages out of Calvin's 'Institutions,' and his explication of the perfidiousness of Valentinus Gentilis, that he might compare them with some passages of the Alcoran, asserting God to be a being of Himself necessarily existing, to whom it is impossible to receive or borrow His essence from another. And thence most uncharitably concludeth, that Mahomet and Calvin must both have had the same wicked design. Episcopius and Curcellæus have been much more modest and candid in animadverting on this novel opinion, and establishing the communicability of the divine nature and essence from the Father to the Son, according to the faith of the Catholic Church."—*Nelson's Life of Bishop Bull*, sect. lvii., pp. 253-257. Oxford, 1816.

Dr. Hook, in his admirable Visitation Sermon, "A CALL TO UNION ON THE PRINCIPLES OF THE ENGLISH REFORMA-

* Symbola tria CATHOLICUM CALVINIANUM LUTHERANUM omnia ipsis eorum verbis expressa. Quirinus Cnoglerus Austrius resensuit et notis illustravit, Colon. 1622

TION," thus expresses himself on the innovating spirit of Calvin :—

"But it was not long before, among the less enlightened friends of the Reformation, a spirit of fanaticism was excited; and acting like the man who continued to whet and whet his knife, until at last there was no steel left in it, they wished to abscind every ordinance, phraseology, and doctrine which might seem to connect them, even indirectly, with Rome, and desired new ceremonies, a new system of theology, a new theological vocabulary, a new Church. And they were not long without a leader, in a man of vast mental powers and of ardent piety, but of an austere temper and strong personal ambition—JOHN CALVIN. Instead of comparing, like our own Reformers and the early Protestants of Germany, the existing system of theology with holy writ and the traditional doctrine of the early Church, he invented an entirely new system of his own, to which, with more than Papal intolerance, he called for a prostration of the judgment, and he proceeded to the length of shedding human blood to support it. Instead of seeking to reform the Church, he was ambitious to build up a sect which might serve as a model to all other religious communions, and over which he seemed willing to usurp such authority as to render it doubtful whether he did not intend to divert to Geneva the appeals which had formerly been made to Rome.

"By Calvin our Prayer Book was denounced as containing fooleries, only tolerable from the exigency of the times, and it was determined to supply its place by a ritual less accordant with the ancient form of worship, and more conformable to the Genevan model. Instead of coinciding with our English Catholic Reformers in their deference to antiquity, they referred, when Scripture was ambiguous or doubtful, to the writings of Calvin, and regarded as heretical all who refused to receive his dogmas as truth." (pp. 13, 14).

Of the *tendency* of Calvin's doctrine of decrees, *his capital innovation in doctrine*, we shall have to make some illustrations in another note.* I shall conclude this with his innovation on Infant Baptism, by giving a forced and erroneous interpretation to that text (John iii. 5), which, until his false gloss, was universally esteemed one

* Note U.

of the strongest foundations of the Christian baptism of infants, as well as adults. I adduce but one passage, and that will suffice, from a learned writer on this subject:—

"All the ancient Christians (without the exception of one man) do understand the rule of our Saviour (John iii. 5)—'Verily, verily, I say unto thee, except a man (it is in the original εαν μη τις, except a person, or except one) be born of water and of the Spirit, he cannot enter into the kingdom of God'—of baptism.

"I had occasion, in the first part, to bring a great many instances of their sayings: where all that mention that text, from Justin Martyr (40), down to St. Austin (300), do so apply it; and many more might be brought. Neither did I ever see it otherwise applied in any ancient writer (1430).* *I believe* CALVIN *was the first*

---

* The editor of the learned work on Infant Baptism inserts the following note at the beginning of the second volume :—

The Rev. Mr. Wall, in the following part of his work, has accommodated his dates to the years after the Apostles, instead of fixing them to the years of our Lord. The dates, therefore, which occur [*between crotchets*] are to be understood as years after *that ever denied this place to mean* BAPTISM.* He gives another interpretation, which he confesses to be new. This man did, indeed, write many things in defence of infant baptism; but he has done ten times more prejudice to that cause by withdrawing (as far as in him lay) the strength of this text of Scripture (which the ancient Christians used as a chief ground of it), by that forced interpretation of his, than he has done good to it by all his new hypotheses and arguments.........Since his time, those parties of the Protestants that have been the greatest admirers of him, have followed him in leaving out this place from among their proofs of infant baptism, and diverting the sense of it another way; which the Antipædobaptists observing, have taken their advantage, and do aim to shut off all the Protestant Pædobaptists from it. They are apt now to face out any of them that make any pretence to this text, as going against the general sense of Protestants."—*The History of Infant Baptism. By W. Wall. Three vols. 8vo. Fourth edition. London, 1810. Vol. ii., pp. 138-140.*

the time of the Apostles; but where two dates are inserted, the first refers to the year of Christ, and the second to the year after the Apostles.

* Institut., lib. iv., c. 16, sect. 25.

Note T, Page 60.

THE SOCINIANISM OF THE CHURCH OF GENEVA.

The following passage, unequivocally declaring the abstinence from discussion, in the pulpit, of the saving and mysterious truths of Christianity, clearly evinces the positive Socinianism of the Genevese ministers, as was alleged of them by Rousseau in these words:—"On demande aux ministres de l'Eglise de Geneve, SI JESUS CHRIST EST DIEU! Ils N'OSENT REPONDRE."

"'The Evangelical Church of Geneva (they say) acknowledges no other guide for its rule of faith than the sacred writings themselves, and positively rejects every human interpretation, simply advising its ministers to avoid the discussion of certain dogmas, or doctrines, which have been the cause of endless disputes ever since the fourth century. The dogmas in question are the nature and divinity of Jesus Christ, and the unity of the Father and the Son; grace; predestination; original sin. When they mention these subjects in their sermons, they confine themselves to simply citing the text of Scripture, without the least commentary. All the ministers, except one, have conformed themselves to this regulation.' Those readers who are versed in the ecclesiastical history of the times of Arius and Athanasius, of the Councils of Nice, of Syrmium, Constantinople, Carthage, &c., as well as in the history of the Reformation, know what storms the discussions of these points have given rise to. These are the very disputes which it is attempted to renew, and which the Genevan ministers wish to decline—after fourteen centuries of fruitless debate. 'It does not appear (they say) that Jesus Christ, or His disciples, ever examined those whom they baptized upon the tenets in question; the precise interpretation of them is not essential to our moral conduct, nor indispensable to us as Christians; in short, if we must yield to any human interpretations, we shall find English theologians to oppose to these same English missionaries, who pretend to dictate a creed to us. Paley, Locke, Clarke, Lardner, and many others, do not hold the same opinions as they do.'

"The ministers of the Church of Geneva state as explicitly what they undertake to teach, as what they do not. The dogmas which they are not averse to discussing from the pulpit are those of divine providence, of the resurrection of the dead, of the last judgment, and of a future state. They teach that Jesus Christ is the promised Messiah, and the Redeemer of mankind; they explain the terms and conditions of this redemption; they insist upon the insufficiency of human reason, and upon the necessity of a divine revelation; at the same time, they lay before their readers the natural evidences of the existence of a Supreme Being, as well as the revealed proofs, both derived from the same source. They think that none of the avenues to the human heart and understanding should be neglected, and that the great object and end of theology is to make revealed religion accord with natural religion."—*Journal of a Tour and Residence in Switzerland, in the years* 1817, 1818, *and* 1819. By L. Simond. Two vols. 8vo. London, 1823. pp. 308-312.

The whole detail of the apostasy of this

community, founded by Calvin, will be found in the pages of the work referred to, which precede and contain the above extract.

The next extract is from the Travels of the present Bishop of Calcutta, and Metropolitan, who declares himself in a preceding letter (X. pp. 289, 290) sufficiently the admirer of this celebrated Reformer. Yet the following is his Lordship's testimony to the present state of things at Geneva:—

"At Geneva, things, I am told, are much worse than here, as to the public doctrines taught by the clergy. The decline in religion began in that city about eighty years back, when the subscription to the formulary of the Swiss Reformers—the noble and most scriptural Helvetic Confession—was abolished; then came in Voltaire, as a resident in the town; next, the Catechism of Calvin was done away with; lastly, a *reglement* was issued about six years since, drawn up with adroitness and caution, but plainly intended to prevent the ministers from preaching explicitly and fully on the divinity of Christ, original sin, grace, and predestination—the three former of which articles contain the very sum and substance of the Gospel; and the latter of which is undoubtedly an important scriptural doctrine. Thus, from being the flower of the Reformed Churches, Geneva has (for the time, and I trust it will be only for a short time) fallen into the gulph of Deism and Socinianism."—*Letters from an Absent Brother, &c.* By Daniel Wilson, M.A., now Lord Bishop of Calcutta, and Metropolitan.

Whether other causes, inherent in the system itself of Calvin, have not contributed to this sad apostasy, I refer the reader to the next note. The doctrine, as taught by Calvin and his followers, of predestination, which, in this sense, I own, I hold to be not only not "an *important* scriptural doctrine," but really not to be a "*scriptural* doctrine"—this doctrine, the most perilous of all the doctrines of the Calvinistic school, contains, it is to be feared, the seeds of scepticism within it.

The entire system is built up with too much of "metaphysical aid." Apostasy has followed.

Note U, Page 60.

TENDENCY OF CALVINISTIC PREDESTINATION, AND LOW CHURCH PRINCIPLES, TO SOCINIANISM; AND THE CONTRARY TENDENCY OF MAHOMETAN HERESIES TO TRINITARIANISM.

" The scheme of the *predestinarian* is different from that *scheme*, nay, even *contrary* to that *scheme*, which the Scripture holds out to us: viz., the economy of man's redemption, founded upon the 'everlasting covenant' of grace and mercy, into which the co-equal and co-eternal *Three*, in the unity of *One Jehovah*, did enter, for us men and for our salvation. No doubt the scheme of the *predestinarian* is founded upon what he is pleased to call the eternal decree of God; but *what* or *whom* the *predestinarian* means by his 'decreeing God' we are never by him distinctly told; whether he means the 'SUPREME BEING,' whom the votary of the religion of nature has fabricated to himself; whether the *sole*

ONE God, whom the Unitarian worships; or whether he means the TRIUNE God, the JEHOVAH ALEIM of revelation. For my own part, the cloven foot of *Socinianism* is to me so visible in this, I shall not say *designedly* restricted mode of expression, that I have ever, on this account, viewed the doctrine which countenances it with becoming abhorrence. Even when the *predestinarian* is constrained to treat of *Christ* and the *Holy Spirit*, as connected with *Deity*, they are represented, for the most part, not as *partners* and *coadjutors* with the '*decreeing God*,' but rather as His '*agents*' and '*instruments*'—the *executors*, in short, of the respective parts assigned to them by the *absolute decree* of God's single and supreme will. This semblance of *inferiority*, although justifiable in its application to the second person in the holy Trinity, in so far as His *assumed humanity* will justify it, ought by no means to be admitted as being applicable to the Holy Spirit, to whom no such assumption, and of course no such semblance of inferiority, belongs: and when, in addition to all this, it is remembered what spirit Calvin was of (the first moulder of *predestination* into its rigid form), who, notwithstanding his professions of orthodoxy, had the audacity to say that the fourth petition of our excellent Litany, 'O holy, blessed, and glorious Trinity,' &c., '*barbariem sapit*,' SAVOURED OF BARBARISM ; and when the modes of expression which his followers make use of are compared with their master's audacious language, something beyond *suspicion* will be found to justify me in presenting the reader with this *objection* to the doctrine which requires, or even seems to require, conformity with the errors of Faustus Socinus."—*Letters addressed to Candidates for Holy Orders.* By the Rev. John Skinner, Episcopal Clergyman, of Longside, Aberdeenshire. Vol. i., pp. 399-401. Aberdeen, 1809.

It has been the opinion of many sound Churchmen, in different periods of the Church since the Reformation, that separation from the Church itself always carries with it a retrograde, or downward tendency to heretical doctrine. We are not aware how many, even of our laity, are preserved from the denial of Christ's divinity, the prime heresy, by our inimitable Book of Common Prayer. I have myself known a congregation, in a town where I was once the clergyman, which had sometimes a Presbyterian minister, and sometimes a Unitarian.* All Low

* Since writing the above, I have met with some striking passages, which strongly confirm both the foregoing note respecting the Church of Geneva, and the remark in this, of Presbyterian Chapels in England, and their congregations, lapsing into Socinianism with the change of a teacher.

"Is it not (asks the excellent Bishop Jebb) a striking fact, that every Reformed Church with which we are acquainted, except our own, has been more or less rapidly verging towards Socinianism?" —*Peculiar Character of the Church of England*: first published as an Appendix to a volume of Sermons in 1815.

The bishop does not, indeed, assign the same reason for this apostasy as has been assigned in the foregoing note; but the fact, whatever may be the cause, is equally appalling.

The Rev. Thomas Bartlett makes the following observations respecting the lapse of English Presbyterians, in his interesting Life of the eminent Bishop Butler:—"It is a painful, as well as a remarkable circumstance, that the larger number of old Presbyterian congregations in England have, since the days of Butler, lapsed into Arianism or Socinianism. The suit and appeals in the case of Lady Hewley's charity have established this fact beyond the power of calling it in question. Possessing neither an authorized confession of faith, nor a legitimate tribunal, as in the Kirk of Scotland, to which they might refer the erroneous statements of their teachers; nor a liturgical service embodying the essential verities of Scripture, with which they might compare them;

Church principles, I firmly believe, have the Presbyterians, in this country (England), were left to be acted upon as the uncontrolled and vacillating views of their instructors might influence their pulpit addresses. And the melancholy result has been, a general defection from the vital doctrine of the Gospel; involving as wide a departure from the principles of the established Presbyterian Church of Scotland, as from those of the Episcopal Church of England."

A passage from the Life of Wilberforce is added in a note—" He confessed (says Mr. Wilberforce, alluding to a conversation he had holden with an eminent Dissenting minister), that not one in twenty of Doddridge's pupils, but who turned either Socinian or tending that way (he himself strictly orthodox); and he said that all the old Presbyterian places of worship were become Socinian congregations."—*Life of Wilberforce*, vol. iii., p. 24. "What an argument (justly observes Mr. Bartlett) is this for a sound scriptural creed! And how should it lead us to thank God for the Articles, Liturgy, and Homilies of the Church of England."—*Life of Bishop Butler*, p. 178.

This subject, in reference to the discussions on Lady Hewley's charity, in the Court of Chancery, is mentioned likewise in an article of *Stephen's (Edinburgh) Episcopal Magazine*, 1836, No. 43, on the Rev. T. Ripland's sermon, "On the Importance of a Liturgy, as a Safeguard to True Religion." It is there stated, in a note, that " out of two hundred and fifty-eight *Presbyterian* congregations in England, two hundred and thirty-five are now *Unitarian*. (See *Eclectic Review*, July, 1832). Of these a large proportion are the descendants of those who, on St. Bartholomew's day, 1632, relinquished, for conscience sake, their livings in the Church." This speaks for itself, and requires no comment.

a TENDENCY to heresy. This is so well expressed by a modern divine, and so entirely accords with my own sentiments, that I shall use his words. Mentioning a public speaker, a sound Churchman, being charged by his adversary with a tendency to Popery, and in turn denouncing the opinions of his opponent, a Low Churchman, as tending to Socinianism or Infidelity:—" For my part (he continues), I am free to confess, that I am opposed to the opinions maintained by those who call themselves Low Churchmen, on this very ground—I believe it to be only on account of their being bad logicians, that they are not Socinians: I believe that they ought to be, if consistent, both Dissenters and Socinians. If they accuse Church principles of tending to Popery, we think that their opinions must lead logical and unprejudiced minds to Socinianism."—*Dr Hook's Call to Union*, p. 48, note.

The maintenance of the Trinity, on the contrary, in the Romish Church, has, perhaps, saved that Church from utter extinction. This is beautifully illustrated by historical facts in the very able and learned work whence my next extract is made. For this pleasing fact I refer the reader to the work itself.

But this writer, Mr. Forster, elicits another very interesting fact, viz., that whereas Christian heresies tend to Socinianism, the heresies of Mahometanism, which is professedly *Unitarian*, tend contrariwise to the true doctrine of the holy and adorable Trinity. The following is this writer's satisfactory statement :—

"In the history of the Church, next in order to the Gnostic heresies must be ranked the whole class of sects which grew up out of a separate debate—the great question respecting the nature of the Godhead, commonly termed the Arian controversy; which, beginning, in the fourth century, with bringing into question the divinity of Christ, advanced, in the end, to the denial of His pre-existence. In every successive age the maintenance of the doctrine of the Divine Unity, in what they pretend to call its first purity, has been the pretext urged, both by the Arian and by the Unitarian heretics, to justify their dissent from the Catholic doctrine of the Trinity,* and their separation from the Catholic Church."

"Now, under the sway of the Mahometan apostasy, where the doctrine of the Divine Unity, as it was speciously miscalled, stood as the great essential article of belief, no room might seem to have been left for the growth of debates or divisions, at all analogous to those which had place in Christendom, upon the mystery of the Godhead. But, however singular, the fact is an ascertained one, that Mahometanism also has had its controversy touching the nature of the Deity; and that the discussions of the fourth century may be seen strangely revived and paralleled, in the disputations which obtained, between the Mussulmans styling themselves orthodox, and the sect of Hayetians, or disciples of Ahmed Ebn Hayet, concerning the character

* For the preservation of the scriptural doctrine, under a divine direction, the Catholic Church owes much to the Athanasian Creed; but for its well-guarded definitions and distinctions, the taint of heresy might have spread in secret, and silently leavened the whole mass.

and nature of Christ.* By this Mahometan doctor, our Lord was affirmed to be, not a mere man, but 'the Eternal Word incarnate,' who 'took upon Him a true and real body, and will judge all creatures in the life to come.' After the example of some Christian heretics, Ebn Hayet, moreover, asserted the doctrine of two gods, or creators of the world—the one eternal, namely, the Most High God; the other non-eternal' namely, the Messiah of the Christians."

"Imperfect and contradictory as were the opinions broached by this Mussulman sectarist, his doctrine of the Godhead, as Mr. Sale has very justly remarked, does not materially differ from the Arian hypothesis; while it is a manifest and decisive advance upon that advocated by the modern Socinians. Nor should that particular aspect of the subject here be lost sight of which gives its peculiar value to this, and to every similar approximation to Catholic truth: the tendency, I mean, of Mahometanism, to assimilate itself to Christianity, through the medium of its reputed heresies. Since, while the heresies of the Christian Church uniformly originated in

* See Pocock, p. 221, &c.

objections to what is mysterious in the scriptural doctrines, the sects accounted heretical among the Mahometans frequently discover, on the contrary, a marked disposition to recognize the great Catholic mysteries. As it may affect the final conversion of the Mahometan world, the circumstance may well be regarded as of the deepest interest and importance; for it argues, in the very nature of Mahometanism, an inherent reaching forth towards an eventual union with the Universal Church of Christ."—*Mahometanism Unveiled.* By the Rev. Charles Forster, B.D., &c. Vol. ii., pp. 103-105. London, 1829.

In a note, the learned author cites an instance, illustrating " the tendency of Mahometan heresy towards Christianity," of " a chief of the Ulemahs, who in the reign of Solyman I. suffered martyrdom rather than renounce his predilection for the Gospel." The narrative, which is in French, is too long for insertion; but I add the author's concluding remark—that " a few more *such* arch-heretics as this noble Turk might shake to its foundations the tottering cause of the Koran. And what Mahometanism has produced, it may produce again."—*Ibid.*, Note O, pp. 501-503.

Note V, Page 67.

THE IMPORTANCE OF PERSONAL RELIGION TO THE MINISTERS OF CHRIST.

I earnestly and affectionately recommend the following touching exhortations of one, well experienced, to the deep consideration of my brethren, the clergy; and I pray God that I also may have grace to profit by them:—

"It is a well-known property of the human mind, that whilst practical habits are strengthened by repeated acts, our passive impressions become weaker by repetition; even as the habituation to danger, which some occupations require, lessens and gradually destroys the impression of fear; and the habitual spectacle of pain or death diminishes, till it annihilates, as we see in several professions, the natural horror with which they are always beheld at first. And from that unchangeable law of our nature it follows, that that close familiarity with sacred and divine subjects, which the ordinary occupations of our profession must occasion, necessarily tends to deaden their impression: and unless active habits of piety have been connected with this service, and grown up with it from the first, their after-production, as the impressions become fainter, is daily less probable, less possible: the man, instead of growing better by the habits of his holy calling, is in the process of becoming incalculably worse. And awful indeed is the case of those to whom, like the insensible priests mentioned by the prophet, who would not hear, nor give glory to the Lord of hosts in their hearts, even their blessings have become cursed; their distinction from the laity in God's house only the seal of their reprobation.* The sinner in the midst of the world, to whom no religious impressions have occurred since those of childhood, which he has forgotten, may be awakened with less expense of means: a word spoken in season, scarcely heeded perhaps by him that uttered it,

---

* Mal. ii. 1, 2.

may have power, through God's grace, to touch his heart with compunction, and remind him of the purer happiness to be obtained in his Father's house: he may return with the prodigal and be accepted. But what word of divine goodness will reach him, who, constantly dwelling in his Father's house, even in the midst of the sanctuary of God, constantly taking his sacred and venerable words into his mouth, yet casts them behind him in his practice, hating to be reformed, and consenting in his heart to the corrupt and evil votaries of the world?* What new means of conviction can be devised for him who habitually frames these into exhortations for others, but not for himself; who speaks with premeditation, from the pulpit, the most awful truths that lie between man and his Maker (for such indeed there are, and sufficient for the humble hearer, in the most indifferent and the coldest sermon), yet who in effect believes them not; whose speech is for custom only, or necessity, or vainglory; the inner springs of hope and fear within him touched exclusively with the objects of sense and the world, or the passions of a heart unsub-

---

* Psalms i., xvi., xvii., xviii.

dued and unreformed? What mysteries of grace can affect him who serves thus before the altar of God—who dispenses the consecrated symbols of divine love and condescension, without discerning, without regarding, the Lord's body, whom his sin crucifies afresh and puts to open shame—who counts thus the blood of the covenant, wherewith he was sanctified, an unholy thing—and turns that bread of life, which is the nutriment of the faithful soul to eternal life, into an opiate of fatal influence to himself, a means of producing that spiritual sickness and slumber which St. Paul mentions as the consequence of such profanation, the lethargy of a hardened conscience and utter forgetfulness of God?* Such is most eminently the unfaithful priest's condition: and though with God nothing is impossible, yet if the impossibility of renovation applies to any case, it surely belongs to this. May that apprehension of its possible existence, with which God has endued the spiritual sense of those who hear me, induce all those whom it concerns to watch and to pray against every approach to a course which issues in a guilt so

* 1 Cor. xi. 29, 30, coll Heb. vi. x. 29.

aggravated, so irremediable."—*Dr. Mill. An Ordination Sermon:—"The Duties of an Apostolical Ministry."* Preached at St. John's Cathedral Church, Calcutta, on Palm Sunday, April 4th, 1830, pp. 30-36.

Note W, Page 69.

DIRECTIONS AS TO THE CONDUCT OF THE NATIVE MINISTERS IN THE CONVERSION OF, AND MINISTRATION AMONG, THE NATIVE INHABITANTS OF CEYLON (COMMUNICATED BY A NATIVE CLERGYMAN).*

To native ministers engaged in the Christian vineyard of this country it would not, perhaps, be improper to offer the following remarks.

The natives of Ceylon are not essentially different, in their general character, from those whom the Apostles addressed, having

---

* The name of the talented writer of this excellent paper is suppressed at his own special request, but with much reluctance on the part of the author and compiler of this Appendix.

in their hearts the same natural propensities to violence and vice; due allowance being made, of course, for the peculiarities arising from local circumstances, which cannot fail to impart a corresponding complexion to their mode of thinking. Neither do *modern* ministers appear to differ from the Apostles, except that they want those extraordinary gifts possessed by the latter. An established Christian government gives to modern ministers some advantages over the Apostles in their *personal security;* but thiss ecurity has, at the same time, some *disadvantages* with respect to personal religion, inasmuch as such security often tends to produce a decay of inward personal piety, by causing the mind to relax in vigilance. It should, therefore, be the primary duty of every minister, under the circumstances, ever to keep this danger in mind, and to attend strictly to the duties of the closet, and to regulate with scrupulous care his private walk with God.

He who is careless in the closet, will be also negligent abroad.

In directing the minister's attention, next, to the great work of conversion, several difficulties would seem to present themselves, *in limine*, to oppose the progress of Christianity. Of these, the principal ones are, the ignorance of the generality of natives, and their consequent incapacity to weigh reason and argument—their superstition, which is the natural result of ignorance—and, in the case of nominal Christians, who compose by far the greatest proportion of the maritime inhabitants, the great apathy and indifference engendered in their minds with respect to Christianity, from their having adopted it merely from worldly motives, and heard it frequently preached and talked of, without the means of thorough conviction of its truth, until it has ceased to be a novelty.

These difficulties, against which a minister has to bear up, are indeed very trying. That which offers the greatest discouragement is the case of nominal Christians who are known to be in reality heathens, and of those professed heathens who already possess some knowledge of the outlines of Christianity. In addressing congregated people of this description, the routine of Christian instruction has no longer the adventitious yet powerful end of novelty in its favour. The apathy, the insensibility to moral appeals, the deadness of heart to religious considerations, which are known to characterize the general mass of the native population, have ceased to be operated upon, in their case, by the excitement of what was once *new*. The doctrines, history, and arguments of Christianity are pretty widely known among them; the preaching of various missionaries, and tracts extensively distributed, as well as the different Christian schools in their vicinity, have left them no longer absolutely ignorant of the great outlines of our divine faith. Curiosity has consequently no food; the motive of gain we do not, would not, dare not offer; self-originated desire for instruction is hardly to be met with; conscience is torpid; the moral sense dull; superstitious belief has blinded the judgment, that it cannot discern the face of truth; and duty only—lingering faith, slow to abandon a hope which God's own word imparts, the yearnings of the heart over the debased, demoralized, and contented victims of such unholy and degrading and destructive systems as Budhism and Gentuism, enable a Christian minister to continue labouring with any tolerable measure of courage and energy under the accumulated depression occasioned by such a concurrence of trials. If he could consent to put up the Lord's stamp on base coin, he might no doubt have no very limited number of others added to that of the already existing nominal Christians.

One circumstance, however, there is, on

which, if improved to advantage under the divine blessing, the Christian minister may build some hope of ultimate success. It is this: that the ignorance of the generality of natives, the fruitful source of all the other evils which it carries in its train, though indeed *very great*, is nevertheless but the result of accidental circumstances, not of any inherent want of natural abilities, of which they possess a great share, requiring only due exercise for their full development. To this circumstance, therefore, the native minister must direct his chief attention. He must, upon favourable opportunities, often seized on for the purpose, endeavour to excite in them a spirit of enquiry. He must next inculcate upon their minds, by a course of plain reasoning suited to their various capacities, the fundamental principles of natural religion, and thus conduct them through the wonderful works of nature, to behold the majesty of nature's God. Original sin, the value of souls, man's utter inability to save himself, and the consequent necessity of a mediator, must form the succeeding topics. These truths cannot be too strongly urged upon the natives, as, without a due sense of them, they can never be brought to a state of salvation. And, finally, after the mind has been thus gradually prepared to shake off the bigotry of superstition, and to receive impressions of rational conviction, he is to usher in, supported by the combined evidence of divine and human testimony, the transcending doctrine of man's redemption, as revealed under the Gospel dispensation, by Christ and Him crucified. The awfully mysterious nature of the Deity, the Triune Jehovah, together with the distinct offices of the Divine Triad, the infinite price of our redemption, and the consequent love and gratitude we owe to Christ, the operations of the Holy Ghost, who is the interior Advocate to whose guidance the Christian is left, the necessity of praying for preventing and co-operating grace, must be unfolded to them in due course. The monstrous idea, encouraged by the various systems of local religion, that the truth of Christianity may be admitted without disparagement to other religions, must be radically removed; and the people (especially the nominal Christian portion of them) fully convinced, that it is only upon the complete destruction of every other system of religion that the Christian superstructure can be raised. This was the method pursued by the Apostles; and it is by following the very same method, after their example, that the native minister must also hope for success in this country.

He must, at the same time, never lose sight of the fact, that this work is not to be done *negligently*. He must be earnest, persevering under all difficulties and discouragements, and feelingly alive to the importance of the subjects of which he speaks or preaches, without which he can hope to do no good.

In the course of this work, he must

judiciously and cautiously advert to the existing religions of the country, and expose their absurdities; but he is on no account to make intemperate attacks upon them, which will only tend to exasperate the natives, and to defeat his own object.

He must be fully prepared to refute absurd metaphysical assertions when brought forward; but he is to avoid entering upon them as much as possible. Nor is it prudent to lengthen out an argument, as it then becomes only a discussion for victory, and leads to anger, rather than conviction.

He should carefully study the objections generally advanced, by intelligent natives, against revelation, in order to be fully prepared to meet them. The creation of our first parents under a liability to transgress—the creation of the devil, and the permission given him to exercise power among men—the promiscuous distribution of good and evil—the circuitous method of human salvation under the mediatorial system, when, as they say, it might have been effected by a simple and independent volition of the Deity: these, and others usually brought forward by infidels in Europe, and often and often refuted by the champions of Christianity, are likewise the objections made by the natives here.

The most effectual method of communicating instruction to the ignorant natives is by familiar conversation. When addressing them from the pulpit, plain expositions of Scripture are more suited to them than argumentative discourses. But, in either case, it is important to get into a right method of doing it; for, though truth lies in the Bible, it is by *man's* means that it remains to be applied to the conscience. Consequently the manner of communicating it must be plain, authoritative, winning, and effective in changing the character.

The native minister must also be careful to govern his temper, and to be courteous and affable in his deportment, which will have much influence with the people he has to deal with; but which, if neglected, will tend to injure his character in no small degree. The same is also necessary to be observed at home, as it will be much effected abroad through the servants, with whom he must know that his conduct is a subject of common conversation. The nature of servants here cannot but be well known to all who have the least local experience.

When entering upon a field where Christianity already exists, he must be careful to observe, as far as possible, the course adopted by his predecessors, and make no innovations, but with great caution.

By pursuing this course with diligence, perseverance, and prayer, it is to be hoped that many a wanderer may be ultimately brought, under the divine blessing, within the sheepfold of Christ. Nor can the minister's labours end here. He will now, on the contrary, have to exercise a strict watchfulness over the conduct of his converts, to commend or reprove, as occasion may require; to guard them perpetually from being corrupted by the surrounding heathen so as to fall away from the faith; to confirm their faith in the truth already received; to pray with them for assistance from above; to exhort them to prayer and watchfulness, and to the exercise of the Christian graces; and thus, by giving them a practical conviction of the excellence of Christianity, in comparison of the divine purity and all-sufficiency of which every other system of mere human invention sinksinto nothingness, he must secure their permanent stability in the faith which followed from sincere conviction.

The foregoing remarks apply only to the grown-up portion of the present native population of the island; but it is to the superior mental acquirements and civilization to be attained by the rising generation, by affording them suitable means of instruction, that we must look forward for the greatest triumphs of Christianity in this semi-heathen land. δ.

These excellent directions I commend seriously to the conscientious consideration, not only of the native clergy ordained upon the occasion, which gave rise to this publication, but to every native clergyman in the island.

Note X, Page 69.

THEOLOGICAL STUDIES.

The dangers of the Church thicken around us, like dark and menacing clouds betokening storm, in almost every direction in which the spiritual eye is turned. We know not what ourselves, more especially the rising generation of clergy, may have to encounter. To arm them for the battle, next to prayer and personal piety, sacred learning must be sedulously cultivated.

But the order of our researches, as we have all experienced who are of any standing in the Church, is a very formidable difficulty to young students. The study of theology seems to divide itself into four parts:—1. Natural religion; 2. Revelation; 3. The Scriptures of the Old and New Testament containing what is revealed; 4. The government of the Church. Some years ago I had occasion to draw up some questions in theology, which were thus divided. I submit them with considerable diffidence, merely as suggestions, to guide the student in the main objects of his research. Books will be easily found. I should, however, recommend but very few on each head, at first, as foundations. They may subsequently be enlarged almost *ad infinitum:* for we have admirable works on all these subjects, and new ones are daily accumulating. But the advice of the younger Pliny will stand the test of all time, and should be rigidly followed by young students in the science of theology, the noblest of all sciences—MULTUM LEGENDUM EST, NON MULTA.

QUESTIONS IN THEOLOGY.
NATURAL RELIGION.

1. What is natural religion, as distinguished from revelation?
2. Can the existence of God be demonstrated upon the principles of natural religion?
3. How would you prove, against the philosophical infidel, that God is a person, and not a principle inseparable from the works of nature, or nature itself?
4. If God be a person, why may He not be corporeal, and composed of matter?
5. What are the natural attributes of God?
6. Can they be demonstrated from the nature of God?
7. What is the distinction between the knowledge and wisdom of God?
8. Is the term "laws of nature" proper?
9. If improper, why?
10. Can the unity of God be demonstrated on the principles of natural religion?

11. Is there any demonstrative proof why more agents than one might not be employed in the works of the creation?
12. How would you prove the world to be governed by a general Providence?
13. Is there a particular Providence?
14. Can God govern empires by a particular Providence without altering the natural course of things?
15. Can He govern the minds of men without affecting the freedom of the human will?
16. Is the soul of man naturally immortal?

REVELATION.

17. Can man arrive at the knowledge of God, or of his own destiny, by the force of his own natural faculties?
18. By what means does or can he arrive at these great and important truths?
19. Does St. Paul, in Rom. i. 20, inculcate the doctrine of natural religion independent of revelation?
20. When, and by what means, did God first reveal Himself to man, and what truths did He reveal?
21. In what manner, and by what means, did God subsequently reveal His will to man?

THE SCRIPTURES—OLD TESTAMENT.

22. Who is the great prophet of the Old Testament?
23. Of what books do his writings consist?
24. Of what great person is Moses the type?
25. Which is the first prophecy of Christ in the Old Testament?
26. By what name does Moses prophesy the coming of the Messiah?
27. Are we, as Christians, absolved from the whole law of Moses?
28. What part is still binding?
29. Was Christ predicted by others of the Hebrew prophets?
30. Will you refer to some of the principal prophecies of His advent?
31. By what titles is He denominated by these prophets?
32. Is the divinity of Christ implied by any of these titles?
33. Can the plurality of the Godhead be proved from the Old Testament?
34. Is there any text of the Hebrew Scriptures which implies a Trinity of persons?
35. What was the nature of the Jewish government?

NEW TESTAMENT.

36. What space of time intervened between the Canons of the Old and New Testament?
37. How was Daniel's prophecy of the seventy weeks fulfilled in the advent of Christ?
38. Was any such person as Christ expected about the period of His advent, by the Hebrews, and by other nations?
39. How did Christ prove His divine mission?
40. How did He prove Himself a Prophet?
41. What other offices, beside the prophetic, did Christ fulfil?
42. By what texts in the Gospels is the divinity of Christ asserted?
43. By what texts in the Epistles is His divinity asserted?
44. How do you prove the personality of the Holy Ghost?
45. How do you prove His divinity?
46. By what texts in the New Testament is the Trinity of Persons in the Unity of the Godhead asserted?
47. What was the purpose of St. John's Gospel?
48. Why do we find the divinity of the Son more insisted on by St. John than by the other Evangelists?

49. How does the text, John xii. 41, verify a passage in the Old Testament, and incontestibly prove the divinity of Christ?

50. By whom were the Acts of the Apostles written?

51. By what authority did the Apostles choose Matthias in the place of Judas, before the descent of the Holy Ghost?

52. By what text in the Acts of the Apostles is it to be shown that the laity have no authority to appoint and ordain the clergy?

CHURCH GOVERNMENT.

53. Why do you present yourself for ordination to a bishop, rather than to any other official person, or community of Christians?

54. How do you prove the divine institution of Episcopacy?

55. What were the ancient names of bishops in the primitive Church?

56. What is Epaphroditus called in the original of St. Paul's Epistle to the Philippians, ii. 25, in relation to that people—and what do you infer from it?

57. What bishops are to be found in the New Testament?

58. Who was the first Bishop of Jerusalem?

59. Are not "bishop" and "presbyter" sometimes used, the one for the other, in the New Testament?

60. How is the authority of a bishop, as the first governor of the Church, to be proved rather than that of presbyters?

61. Is there any, and what, analogy between the Jewish and Christian priesthood?

62. How many orders of clergy are mentioned in the New Testament?

63. Do the various spiritual gifts enumerated by the Apostle, 1 Cor. xii. 8, 9, 10, constitute so many orders of clergy?

64. How many orders of clergy are designated in that chapter?

65. What is meant by the angels of the Seven Churches in the Apocalypse?

SUPPLEMENT.

Many interesting publications, on subjects treated of in the foregoing pages, have appeared since the Sermon was published and the Appendix drawn up. Extracts from some of these will be found in the first three numbers of the following SUPPLEMENT. The fourth number will explain itself.

COLOMBO, *April* 7, 1843.

SUPPLEMENT.

I.

APOSTOLICAL SUCCESSION.

"Our blessed Lord gave to His Apostles a general commission to build His Church, and a promise of the Holy Spirit to guide them in all things necessary for the due execution of their all-important task, as well as an assurance of His own continued presence with the ministry even to the end of the world. Under that authority, and with the certainty of that guidance, the holy Apostles *did* proceed to construct the Church, according to a certain form of polity; which, as being of Apostolical origin and authority, was observed by the universal Church, in all its branches for many ages; so that it was never even thought of, that there could be a *Church* without a *bishop;* nor that any persons should claim authority to minister the word and sacraments who had not been ordained by a bishop.

"The doctrine of an Apostolical succession in the ministry is asserted by the Presbyterian divines, as well as by ourselves, only *they* maintain that the ministerial commission has descended through a succession of *presbyters;* we, that it has come to us through a line of *bishops;* and that we have the testimony of all history on our side, I think has been already proved. If, then, the Episcopal form of Church government be undoubtedly Apostolical in its origin and authority; if the right and the duty of preaching the word of truth and dispensing the sacraments of grace have been transmitted through that channel, from the holy Apostles themselves, to the ministers of Episcopal Churches; it cannot be otherwise than presumptuous and hazardous for men to turn away their eyes from that pattern, and to separate themselves, or to live in a state of separation, from a Church which can exhibit these credentials of its spiritual authority, and against which none of those charges can be brought, which alone justify separation; and it ought to be a subject of devout thankfulness to those who belong to such a Church, that at least there can be no question as to the commission of its ministers, and their right to dispense the sacraments—no question, I mean, as between *them* and the ministers of any congregations not being Episcopal: seeing that whatever reasons may be urged for the validity of *their* mission, apply with still greater force to ours."*—*Three Sermons on the Church, preached in the parish Church of St. James, Westminster, during Lent,* 1842. By Charles James, Lord Bishop of London, pp. 50, 51.

ON SEPARATION; AND THE STATE OF FOREIGN CHURCHES.

"But before we proceed with the enquiry, I wish to point out the difference which exists, as to the bearings of this subject, between those

---

* Generally speaking, it is unsafe to argue *a facto ad jus*, so as to conclude peremptorily the one from the other. But we are certainly warranted in saying, that what the Apostles did in the matter of Church government, is the best pattern that we can have, and that it is safer to adhere to than depart from it. I will add here, what I ought, perhaps, to have stated in the Sermon itself, that we are not to confound the simple question of the government of the Church by bishops, with those which concern the extent or limitation of their jurisdiction, or the supremacy of one bishop over another: this former may have been of Divine or Apostolical institution— the latter of positive order, agreed upon amongst Christians.

persons who separate themselves from a national Church, which is beyond question, in all essentials, a branch of the Church Catholic—for instance, our own—and those who are members of national Churches, or congregations, not under Episcopal government; as, for example, the inhabitants of those countries on the continent of Europe where the Reformed religion prevails, as to doctrine, but where the government of the Church is not, as we believe, Apostolical. It may be possible, and we believe it to be true, that the former incur the guilt of schism, from which the latter are exempt. The former cannot allege any of the reasons which alone can justify separation from a particular Church—that it practices idolatry; that it teaches doctrines contrary to the fundamentals of Christian faith, or to the laws of Gospel holiness; that it will not admit them to communion without their doing something forbidden, or professing something untrue; or, lastly, that it is itself in a state of schism from the true Church. None of these accusations can they prove against the national Church of this realm, and therefore they are themselves guilty of schism in separating from it. But the members of any one of the other

Reformed, non-Episcopal Churches, to which I have alluded, do *not* separate themselves from *any* Churches; nor, if they quitted their own Churches, is there any Episcopal Church in their country to which they could unite themselves; and therefore, as long as their own Church holds the essentials of doctrine, they may continue therein, and are in no sense schismatics. Their own Church may not be in that perfect communion with the Catholic Church which would subsist if there were a unity of discipline as well as of doctrine: it may be the duty of their Church to desire that unity, and to take steps for its restoration; and it may be the duty of individual members of that Church to promote that happy consummation by all prudent and peaceable methods; but in the mean time, not thoroughly knowing what may be the impediments which block up the way to Catholic unity, and of necessity render the progress therein tedious and difficult, I dare not pronounce that Church to be cut off altogether from the mystical body of Christ; and I am sure that none of its *members* are chargeable with the guilt of schism who do not thwart and impede the efforts of the Church itself to assimilate its government and discipline to the Apostolical model.

"That the Apostolical model *ought* to be followed by every *local* Church, I have no manner of doubt; nor that its adoption is absolutely necessary to the Church's perfectness and efficiency as a dispenser of truth and grace. But if I find entire branches of the great Christian family living under a different form of government, deprived of the advantages of Episcopacy, in the first instance not by their own fault, but through the tyranny and obstinacy of the Church of Rome refusing them those advantages; being also in that state of dependence upon the secular power which was occasioned by the want of a legitimate spiritual government, and from which, by their own mere motion, it is difficult, if not impossible, to extricate themselves: I cannot consent to speak of those communities as being altogether aliens from the Church of Christ, nor to deal with them as though they were entirely destitute of the privileges which belong to it. I pity and lament their want of some of those privileges; and I pray that *they* too may *feel* that want, and that the Great Head of the Church may bring them into the full perception and enjoyment of those privileges; but I dare not *think* of them, still less *speak* of them, as heretics or schismatics—I dare not pronounce them, as such, excommunicate; and I tremble at the arrogance and uncharitableness which presume to deal out anathemas against those who deny no one fundamental point of faith, but who are defective (it may be questioned whether by their own fault) in the form of their government, and, as connected therewith, in the clear and indisputable succession of their ministry."—*Ibid.*, pp. 53-56.

FOREIGN CHURCHES NOT HERETICAL AND SCHISMATICAL.

"For these reasons, it is admitted, by those of our divines who take the highest ground in asserting the claims of Episcopacy, that the earlier Lutherans and Calvinists were not heretics nor schismatics. If so, I would desire to be told, at what period of time their descendants became so? I know very well that it is not difficult to trace, in the history of their Churches, the gradual declension of orthodoxy, and to point out the individual writers who became, in succession, more and more heretical in their teaching, till they were plunged into that dismal gulf of rationalism, below which there is hardly a lower depth to reach. And I know, too, that this was a consequence, perhaps a punishment, of the imperfect system of Church government which was suffered to remain so long after the first necessity had passed away. But I will not venture to say, that because this or that generation of men did not re-establish that perfect community with the Catholic Church, in ecclesiastical discipline, which had been forcibly interrupted, not by *their* fault, therefore they and those who came after them, and who were probably less able to take that step, are to be considered as schismatical, it being admitted that their forefathers, who lived under the same form of Church government, were not so. As Churches, they are undoubtedly defective; wanting some of those privileges and securities which are enjoyed, in all their completeness, by those Churches which are, and always have been, constituted according to the Apostolic model: but to their individual members I dare not deny a participation in all things required of necessity to salvation.

"It appears to me, that, in this manner, it is by no means difficult to reconcile *truth* with *charity*—to hold a firm conviction of the Apostolical origin and constitution of our own Church, with a persuasion, or at least a charitable hope, that those national Churches which, having once unavoidably and unwillingly lost the perfectness of ecclesiastical order, have not yet regained it, possibly not having been able to do so, are yet within the pale of Christ's Church—so far, at least, as the being so is necessary to the final salvation of their individual members. 'Although I see (says Hooker) that certain Reformed Churches, the Scottish especially, and French, have not that which best agreeth with the sacred Scripture I mean the government—that is by bishops—this their defect and imperfection I had rather lament in such a case than exagitate, considering that men oftentimes, without any fault of their own, may be driven to want that kind of polity or regimen which is best, and to content themselves with that which either the irremediable error of former times, or the necessity of the present, hath cast upon them.'* The necessity of which he speaks, whether it exist or not with respect to entire Churches or communities, may exist with respect to all the members of such churches who bear no rule therein, nor

---

* Eccl. Pol., iii. 11.

have power to change their form of government. The more exclusive view of the subject, which peremptorily shuts out all such Christian communities from the true Church, and treats them as heretical and schismatical, I consider to be more in accordance with the intolerant arrogance which breathes in the decrees of the Council of Trent, than with the wise and pious caution that pervaded the Synod of our own Church which framed her articles of faith. It is said, indeed, that those holy and prudent men were purposely wary and reserved in their definitions of Church government, for fear of giving offence to the foreign Reformed Churches. I believe their caution to have proceeded rather from a religious fear of deciding peremptorily that which is not peremptorily decided in the word of God, and of excluding from any of the benefits of the Christian economy those who have not been formally excluded therefrom by Jesus Christ and His Apostles. Almighty God may do what He will with His own. We know what He hath given *us*; and *how* He gives it; let us value it and be thankful for it as we ought. But if it please Him to give the same benefit to others in a somewhat different method, shall we deny *them* the right of receiving it, or question *His power* to give it? *Is our eye evil, because He is good?*"*—*Ibid*, pp. 58-62.

The only possible objection to the argument of the above learned and right reverend writer is that which is suggested by himself in this third and last extract; that "the gradual declension of orthodoxy," in these Churches, may without difficulty be traced, until, in his own powerful language,

"The writers *became, in succession, more and more heretical in their teaching, till they were plunged into that dismal gulph of rationalism, below which there is hardly a lower depth to reach.*

---

* Our Reformers, in the Book of Consecration, approved in the Thirty-sixth Article, insist strongly upon the necessity of Episcopal ordination—a point which Bishop Sanderson says " has been constantly and uniformly maintained by our best writers, and by all the sober, orderly, and orthodox sons of the Church ;" but they do not presume to say that it is impossible, under any circumstances, for a Church to exist without it. We may, however, set their formal approval of the Consecration Book against the private opinions of Archbishop Cranmer, in his answers to the ninth question concerning Church government.

AND I KNOW, TOO, THAT THIS WAS A CONSEQUENCE, PERHAPS A PUNISHMENT, OF THE IMPERFECT SYSTEM OF CHURCH GOVERNMENT WHICH WAS SUFFERED TO REMAIN SO LONG AFTER THE FIRST NECESSITY HAD PASSED AWAY."

If the reader have attentively followed the compiler of this APPENDIX in the arrangement of his facts, he cannot fail to perceive, that the argument of the long departure from the visible Church, judicially punished by GOD in their confirmed heresy, is never lost sight of. The independent witness to THE SAME FACT, by so powerful a mind as that of the Bishop of London, in a work published nearly three years after these papers were drawn up, is no unimportant corroboration of the almost unavoidable truth of this melancholy, but too just conclusion.

II.

UNION OF THE WORD OF GOD AND THE CHURCH OF GOD.

The Right Rev. George Washington Doane, Bishop of New Jersey, in America, recently visited England, on the invitation of Dr. Hook, the Vicar of Leeds, to preach the sermon at the consecration of the new church at Leeds. On his return to America, the bishop preached and published a sermon, entitled, " The glorious things of the City of God," containing his " impressions of the Church of England." 1842. In the Appendix to this very interesting sermon are printed some valuable documents, giving an account of the author's reception at public meetings of the clergy, or where the clergy chiefly acted and presided. Among others are the proceedings of the sixth annual meeting of the Coventry Religious and Useful Knowledge Society, at which the Rev. Dr. Hook,

Vicar of Leeds, was in the chair. From the American bishop's speech on this occasion I cannot but transcribe the following interesting and admonitory facts and reflections, which are quite in unison with the leading principle of this publication :—

"It were easy to show from the holy Scriptures, and from the ancient fathers, that the word of God and the Church of God were joined together of God, and therefore not by man to be put asunder. One is the witness of the other. What has been the effect of separating the Scriptures from the Church? What has been the effect in Germany and Switzerland? Where are those who started on the principles of the Reformation, yet separated themselves from the Church? Where are their sound religious principles? Where is their faith? What is it? I have lived in a land peopled by those who emigrated from this country. It is the fashion to call some of them the 'Pilgrim Fathers'—men who fancied themselves somehow straitened in the enjoyment of religious liberty—who, in the claim of greater freedom in

God's worship and service, set out for distant shores, and planted themselves in a region now called New England. I enter not into the enquiry as to the character of these men—the justice of their complaints, or the motives for their proceedings. I will accord to them all that charity can ask. They went from here, as they thought and truly believed, the true followers of the Gospel of Jesus Christ; preaching, as they thought, the very principles of the Reformation, but without a Church, without a Liturgy—with no transmitted authority from God to minister in holy things. They were self-denying, laborious men. Almost the first thing they did was to found a college for the education of persons as Gospel preachers. They have every claim to our admiration for their devotedness to their cause. They denied themselves the comforts of life for the establishment of this institution. For a while, it went on, more or less, according to their expectations; but after a time, the institution, which they planted as a nursery for preachers of Christ and Him crucified, became, and has been for years, a nursery for Unitarianism. Nor is that the worst. They have gone far beyond this stage of incipient putrescence. The rankest enormities of doctrine are now rife among the descendants of the 'Pilgrim Puritans' that ever festered on the face of the earth. And the men who themselves forwarded the theological school at Cambridge, and who boast in themselves, as Unitarians, amazed and terrified at the fruits of their hands, Pantheism and Atheism, would be glad to see the institution crumbled into dust. THIS COMES OF THE SEPARATION OF GOD'S TRUTH FROM GOD'S CHURCH. To prevent the evil we must forbid the divorce."

Another speaker at this meeting, the Rev. H. Townsend Powell, remarked, in reference to the above extract of Bishop Doane's speech, as follows:—

" One question had been most beautifully illustrated by his lordship in his address, that the Church was not only the keeper of the holy word, but the witness to its true interpretation. They well knew there must be an interpreter of the holy word, as well as a keeper; but the question was, in what way was that interpretation to be handed down to them. If they set up the authority of the Church, so as to make it the judge, they would fall into the error of Romanism; but the only safe way was to keep to the words used that evening—that the Church was the only witness to the true interpretation of the Scriptures. That has been the case uniformly pursued by the Church. It was that principle which had been so beautifully illustrated, and he tendered his humble thanks to his lordship for putting him in possession of such a clear view of the case. He, being a bishop of the one Catholic Church, in a distant land, had, by his presence among them, realized the nature of a Christian society existing there. While they contemplated the Church at a distance, it was but a sort of theoretic idea; but when part of that component body was present, they knew what the Church really was. The Church, whether in England, or three thousand miles distant, was the same, and proceeded at first from the Church at Jerusalem. They had heard how the Church in America felt its destitution for want of a bishop. They applied to England for the Episcopal succession, which was granted; so that they were now one—not one in external superstructure—not merely as a body compacted together, as bone to bone—but one in name, one in heart, one in principle, one in love; and wherever the same language extends, the same faith extends also. Then, should they not feel for one another as brethren? He would say to his lordship, and the other reverend gentlemen who had addressed them—take back this union of hearts of Englishmen. They were Churchmen, and, though distant from each other, existed in one bond of union, which would be a blessing through life and to all eternity."

III.

THE REFORMATION, PRESBYTERIANISM, AND EPISCOPACY.

Events in England, especially during the last three years, have year by year, and month by month, forced these important subjects into notice and discussion. At this distance we hear MORE than "a confused noise of battle," and conflict of antagonist views on these questions; and what greatly stirs the mother-country and the mother-Church must be felt in the colonies, and the Churches therein planted.

The collision of opinion is exhibited in a form the most satisfactory, namely, the republication of works of our English Reformers; translations of foreign works on the continental Reformation; the examination of public documents respecting the Protestant Church in France; and, lastly, to bring the question still more home to the business and bosoms of Englishmen, the works or tracts of the Anglican Fathers, now in the course of republication. The two great principles of Church government, which have divided the Reformed Churches, and which alone claim any divine commission, as of Apostolic descent, and therefore alone worthy of notice—EPISCOPACY and PRESBYTERIANISM, as accredited witnesses of the true faith—are tested by these republications. Another mode of testing them is the contest now carrying on in Scotland between the Presbyterian Establishment and the Civil Government; the effect of which has been a silent, unobtrusive, but a very decided and considerable increase of the numbers of that body which is emphatically OUR SISTER CHURCH, THE EPISCOPAL CHURCH OF SCOTLAND.

The view of these subjects will be best exhibited by transcribing some paragraphs from a *Review* decidedly of Church principles, but now moderate, and holding the *via media* between the two extremes (for at first it was of the ultra-Protestant party, but has long been in other and better hands)—the *Church of England Quarterly Review*—selected from articles published between 1840 and 1842.

1. "It is, we believe, more to the different direction of their studies, than to the circumstances of the case, that the continental Reformation went on, in defiance of Apostolical discipline, and that in this country in accordance therewith; for, had the Reformed congregations on the continent desired it, they could, even in the reign of Henry VIII., have had canonically

consecrated bishops. Who could doubt the willingness of Cranmer, Ridley, and Latimer, to have conferred such consecration upon persons properly recommended to them for the purpose? The title would have involved no lordship—no dominion—no revenues; it would but have placed them in the position of the Anglo-American bishops of our own day, who were similarly consecrated; but the truth was, they were earnest only for doctrine, and careless about discipline. They were not aware of what, had they been diligent students of Church history, they would clearly have been, viz., that there *cannot long be purity of* DOCTRINE *without apostolicity* of DISCIPLINE, and they were soon to experience the truth of this neglected aphorism.

" Nearly contemporaneous with Ridley, arose in France a man whose name has now become historical. In 1509 was born John Calvin, and in 1536 he published his 'Institutes.' The haughty and ambitious character of the man, his learning and eloquence, his fervent zeal for the Reformation, soon made his influence felt; and it was not long before he established himself as a Protestant Pope at Geneva. Here he contrived the consistorial scheme of Church government, constituting himself perpetual president, and ruling the 'Reformed Churches,' as they were called, with a rod of iron. His doctrines, which were borrowed from Augustine, he explained in a remarkably lucid manner, and his phraseology has gradually been adopted by all Presbyterians and Dissenters: even those who repudiate his theory of predestination, take his opinions and his peculiar phraseology (which was *not* that of the primitive Church) in other points; and, as might be expected, in many cases the acceptance of the doctrines soon followed the acceptance of the language. We have, in other places, shown that his personal influence in this country was never very perceptible, and that the Seventeenth Article, and some others, were drawn up with reference to other tenets; that, in truth, the earlier Reformers looked to *Germany* for aid in developing the *doctrines*, and to the *fathers* in developing the *discipline*, of the Church. Yet some, who visited or were banished to the continent, imbibed the predestinarian theory, and among these was Grindall, successively Bishop of London, Archbishop of York, and then of Canterbury. Bradford and Hooper, too, were not without a tincture of the same doctrine; and it is probable that one of the greatest losses which the divinity of that period suffered was the loss of Ridley's 'Treatise on Election,' addressed to Bradford. Whitgift, again, entertained the same views, and they became more common in his age, and the one which succeeded him. But in that which preceded him there were only Bradford and Hooper among men of note who were predestinarians. This— viz., Calvinism—was the first disturbing force acting upon the Reformation. The Marian persecution had been a fierce onslaught, but when it passed away, the principles of the Reformed remained the same, even though their number was diminished. Calvinism, however, acted from within: its theory is most plausible; it rests upon an apparent search into the Scriptures, but it is a search in which the investigator relies on his own metaphysical subtlety, and rejects the testimony of the united Church till the age of St. Augustine. It entails consequences which neutralize all appeal to antiquity, and brings with it a phraseology contradictory at once to the Anglican formularies and the doctrines of the Apostolic era. There are few things which have had so injurious an effect on the condition of our Church as the adoption by the Evangelical *party* (we speak here advisedly, for there are, thank God, many truly Evangelical men who are not connected with the party)—we say, then, that few events have done more mischief than the adoption, by the Evangelical *party*, of the Genevan phraseology. It has, in the minds of many, become identified with true religion; and the individual who should say that he was ' regenerated in his baptism, made a member of Christ, a child of God, and an inheritor of the kingdom of heaven,' would be immediately set down as something very like a heathen, if not much worse, viz., a Roman Catholic. How many, alas! are there of the clergy who would thus judge, and who deem the absolution to the sick Popish, and yet have solemnly sworn that they give their hearty and unfeigned assent and consent to all that is written in the Book of Common Prayer. Let us put one more home question. How many clergymen are there of the Evangelical PARTY, *who, not being* EVANGELICAL HIGH CHURCHMEN, *can, in this particular, escape the guilt, the awful guilt of* PERJURY! Yet this has altogether arisen from the adoption of the Genevan phraseology."

"But we must, though unwillingly, quit a favourite field of discussion, and shall conclude this paper by a few remarks on the influence exerted by the Swiss and German Reformers here and in their own country. Calvin actually proposed, to all the Reformed communities in Europe, to call together a synod, to consider the possibility of establishing something like an uniformity of worship; but as his known object was that the uniformity should be a Genevan uniformity, Elizabeth instructed him that the English Church would retain her Episcopacy, and his scheme dropped. At various times, attempts have been made to calvinize, doctrinally, the Church in this country; and the nine assertions orthodoxal drawn up at Lambeth are important, because they show that, in the judgment of Calvinistic divines, she was not so at that time. The influence then exercised here by the letters and writings of the great French Reformer have been confined to individuals, and have never been carried out in the formularies of the Church. Our Episcopacy has preserved a regularity of government and a perpetuity of doctrine which we look for in vain in any communion not Apostolically constituted. The Presbyterian form of Church government, which gives a large power to the laity in spiritual matters, tends, of course, to encourage great liberty in interpretation; and it is very natural to suppose, that he who is to sit in judgment on a priest, is also qualified to sit in judgment on a creed: for he obviously has as much Apostolical authority over one as over the other. Gradually have the evil effects of this spiritual republicanism displayed themselves in the deterioration of doctrine; and the greater part of the Reformed communities on the continent are cankered by Socinianism or Neology. We would earnestly exhort all those who have any doubts on the *necessity*—we do not say the expediency—of Episcopacy, to turn to our late articles on 'The State of Protestantism in France,' and 'The Continental Reformation.' Presbyterianism and Episcopacy are now fairly in comparison in Scotland, and it may there be seen that the one contains within itself the seeds of its own dissolution. The principle of religious republicanism is now, under the form of the Veto question, agitating the Scottish Establishment to its foundation; while unestablished, unendowed Episcopacy, though old as Christianity itself, is making steady and rapid progress. It is adapted to all times—accommodates itself to all circumstances. It flourished in imperial England, and would, were the British Government to do its duty, prove the salvation of the country: may it, by God's blessing, be permitted to be! It flourished in republican America, and may be, probably is, the salt that preserves that Government from utter corruption. It flourishes in Presbyterian Scotland, and will, ere long, be the chief form of religion there. Established or non-established (*that* question concerns the *country* only, not the *Church*), endowed or not endowed, encouraged or persecuted, it prospers alike, and will do so; for it is the form of polity established in the Apostolic Church, and that Church is built upon the Rock, even Christ, and the gates of hell shall not prevail against it."—*The Church of England Quarterly Review*, No. xxi., January, 1842. Article: The Parker Society, pp. 11-13, 27, 28.

2 On the continent of Europe the spirit of political anarchy and religious infidelity is and has been in operation ever since that fearful disruption of society, as by the

explosion of a volcano—the French Revolution. Had the Reformation been conducted on the continent generally as it was in England, there would have been a powerful counteracting influence, for which we now look in vain, either from the Church of Rome, which rather spreads than stays the plague, on the one hand, or from the imperfectly reformed Continental Churches on the other. Upon this subject we will extract a paragraph, showing the existing state of things and opinions, from another article of the very respectable periodical already cited:—

" It will be difficult for the attentive observer, who patiently waits for the visible manifestation of God's providence, and who has been led to look at His work in this world as a whole; who is disposed to embrace in one glance the ages past, together with the present elements, and to apply the teaching of past events to future probable results; it is difficult, we say, not to feel persuaded that the question of an Apostolic and truly CATHOLIC EPISCOPACY, in opposition to the Romish corruptions, will, ere very long, become THE GREAT QUESTION IN EUROPE."—*Ibid.*, No. xix., July, 1841. Article: The Reformation on the Continent, p. 128.

If the old countries of Europe, which have for so many ages been converted to at least a nominal Christianity, require these facts and these warnings to be held up to them; if England, which has by God's providence been blessed with a more perfect reformation, retaining her Apostolic and truly Catholic Episcopacy, stands, nevertheless, in need of this admonitory voice, lest SHE fall back into Romanism or schism, surely the possessions, both in the east and west—these Asiatic countries, upon which "the day-spring" of the Gospel is but just beginning to dawn and to spread her light, imperiously demand the right way to be laid open before them.

The writer just cited, after stating the fact of the failure of great and pure-minded men in the great work of the Reformation, though " animated by the love of truth, of holiness, and of eternal things," thus ably developes the causes of their failure :—

"If we look carefully into the causes which finally produced the extinction of so many courageous efforts to establish God's truth, we shall find that it was when man lost sight of the unity of Christ's visible Church, and let go from the means and instruments which secure it. Our Saviour's prayer to the Father was, 'May they be one, as we are one!' This prayer is left for our instruction, and we shall uniformly find, that in proportion as this Catholic feeling has been lost sight of, and the body of Christ rent, there have sprung up the germs of future dissolution among those communions which have forsaken it. Self-complacency and mutual gratulation, though they may blind and delude for a while, cannot set aside the result; neither do they afford any proof of the contrary. That test is supplied by the sanction of the Divine approbation, which can itself be read only through the succession of generations and of centuries.

This is the test which the Reformation in the countries here treated of, Germany and Switzerland, has to withstand; and which it is the duty of *every* Christian, anxious for the extension of the Saviour's kingdom, and especially *our* duty in the present age, *carefully* to weigh and to consider.

"What resulted from the Reformation in those countries remains connected principally with the names of Luther and of Calvin—a circumstance which must at once be felt as indicating a departure from that principle held by the Apostles, not to belong to Paul or to Apollos—a violation, therefore, of the unity then bequeathed, and which it must be evident, even to the superficial observer, is very precious to be maintained. And it is but too common to find, among those who are thus called after these names, that, whatever those Reformers embraced in their labours, all that *they* did and established is adopted and taken account of; whereas, whatever was primitive and apostolic, and existing long before them, is ignorantly or blameably overlooked. Thus those two great institutions —Liturgies and Episcopacy—the stays and bulwarks of universal belief, are lost sight of.

Thus, too, disregard is had to the thought of that universal body of believers, the visible Church, with which every individual believer is, outwardly as well as spiritually, connected; that BODY CATHOLIC is, or is not, living in a bond of communion; that either such one is, or is not, which has subsisted upon earth since the time of its Heavenly Founder and His Apostles.

"It is an acknowledged fact, and, indeed, a matter upon which it is very easy to be satisfied, that separation from this body was *not the spirit* in which Luther himself proceeded. He did not wish to separate from the communion of the Church Universal. At the very time he made that bold appeal from the Pope to the authority of a General Council (a proceeding, be it observed, quite accordant with the practice even in the Romish system), we find him solemnly abjuring any intention of 'departing from the *sentiments of the Church!*' and subsequently adding, that he would not trouble the Church for trifling matters, and would 'submit to all that was required of him for the sake of peace.' This will afford proof how loath was this man of robust faith to originate any separation from the Universal Church. The Lutherans presented, as a body, their Confession of Faith to the Emperor Charles V., at Augsburg. In that Confession they declare they do not wish to transmit to their children and posterity any doctrine different from that of the word of God and Christian truth. 'None of the articles of our faith differ from those of the Catholic Church, but only abuses have been omitted,' &c. (pars ii. prœm). 'According to the Gospel, or *jure divino*, bishops, as such—*i.e.*, those who have the ministry of the word and sacraments—have no other jurisdiction than to remit sins, to take cognizance of doctrine, and to reject doctrine different from the Gospel, and to exclude sinners of known impiety from the communion of the Church, without human force. Hence the Churches ought necessarily, and *jure divino*, to obey them.' (Pars. ii. art. 7).—*Ibid.*, pp. 130, 131.

Melancthon, in his celebrated "Apology of the Confession," breathes the same sentiments. "For (says this great and holy man) I see what a Church we shall have, if we overthrow the ecclesiastical polity." But although Luther and his contemporaries are not ANTI-EPISCOPALIANS; though they would have wished an Episcopacy, and at first received the CREEDS of the primitive Church, and professed to be guided by Scripture and tradition; though the Reformers themselves maintained these doctrines, their successors have not been animated by the same sentiments.

"They have fallen into asserting an unbounded freedom of private judgment; some by degrees took boldness, and, throwing aside the wise moderation of their predecessors, *proclaimed*, as the *essential principle* of the Reformation, the liberty of interpreting Scripture according to the suggestions of their own private judgments, without any reference to the judgment and opinions of the Universal Church in all ages. And we have the grief of beholding, at the present day, communions, as well as individuals, acting as if there had never been any Christianity in the world before, and thinking themselves authorized to hold whatever doctrines they please to devise; who even are found speaking and acting as if there were no other Christians existing besides those who compose their own small bodies. And that order of Episcopacy, which from the beginning—that is to say, for the period of fifteen centuries—had never been called in question, was first set aside and dispensed with at Geneva; the Reformer Beza being himself found ready, at the Colloquy of Poissy, to justify the unauthorized assumption of those sacerdotal functions which, until that time, it had never been held could be exercised, except *by transmission!*

"Thus a new system came to be established, which clearly placed its adherents out of the order and communion of the Universal Church. The unity of the Christian body has been lost sight of by numbers. The Episcopal institution and original liturgies they have suffered to escape from them, and the connecting bonds with primitive Christianity have been deliberately and voluntarily surrendered; and the vessel they have thus embarked in, damaged and weakened by this forcible severing from her primitive holds, through which she could be connected with the eternal, unmoveable *Rock*, has drifted along among shoals and breakers, and has received such injuries as endanger her very existence."—*Ibid.*, p. 133.

"It is certainly with something like a sentiment of awe that, recollecting we nowhere in Scripture read of any one who ordained himself, who took upon himself the office of the ministry, we contemplate those communions which have cast away the idea of Catholicity, and who reject Episcopacy, without sufficiently considering how far any one can be authorized in setting aside an institution of so much authority, merely because some of those appointed to it have at any period fallen into corruption and abuse, and so venture to institute a new ministry, unauthorized, unsent! What though a degenerate branch of the Universal Church, like that of Rome, be foremost in proclaiming its necessity, going even so far as to pretend it exists only within its own pale? Can we be justified in rejecting it, any more than we should be in rejecting so many points of Catholic truth which she still holds; because she has in many cases perverted them, and covered them with rubbish? Shall we throw away the grain because of the chaff? Shall we lose sight of the body of Christ, and have our view so far perverted that a man shall see the Church of Christ among all manner of persons, and even imagine a Church to be incorporated in a single individual?

"Such are the blessings which have been conferred on our National Church of England; such are the dangers she has been preserved from. To her pertains that *afflatus* which our gracious Lord bequeathed with the commission, 'As my Father sent me, so send I you;' and she feels herself, therefore, in a position to be in communion with all those who, having received from the FOUNTAIN HEAD OF TRUTH, through the *Apostles* and *their successors*, the pure doctrine of the Gospel, desire to preserve it unalloyed, and to keep themselves in communion with lawfully appointed governors and pastors. 'And lo! I am with you always:' not with yourselves personally, for I go to prepare the place, that where I am, you may be also; therefore the world cannot long possess you: but *with all* those to whom you shall intrust my doctrine, and who shall be keepers of it in the same manner *after you*, until the end. 'Even Christ glorified not Himself to be made an High Priest' (says the Apostle), but came *commissioned from the Father*, even a voice from heaven proclaiming, 'Hear ye Him,' and the Holy Spirit descending in a visible bodily form, as the Great Bishop and Pastor of His Church came up from the waters of John's baptism. The fundamental principles of our Church are not, therefore, such as cannot stand investigation. They result, in the clearest manner, from the authority of Scripture, with the undeniable confirmation of the practice from the time of the Apostles through all the subsequent centuries. And since all that pertains to truth and godliness, we must expect, will be impugned and arraigned, can it be wondered at that the great adversary, finding that the Church of England (let us not be backward in declaring it) embodies the most perfect ensample of scriptural apostolic truth, should stir up the bitterest enmity and opposition against her, on the part of those who have either corrupted those principles, or who have spurned them? The maxim, 'Divide et impera,' has been too successful a portion of the great tempter's strategy to be abandoned *now*, when, by a very sensible effusion of God's Holy Spirit abroad, so much of his empire is being shaken.

"We have been led into this train of thought from a sense of those fearful evils, *Rationalism* and *Socinianism*, that have deluged divers Reformed portions of Europe, which are still distilling their fatal venom over the present generation; and whose mortiferous stream can be traced up to a departure from Catholic doctrine, Catholic discipline, and Catholic worship."—*Ibid.*, pp. 135, 136).

"On a view of the endless maze of error and novelty in which so many sections of the visible Church have been wandering, members of our Apostolic Church will doubtless have their feelings of thankfulness excited for possessing such safeguards and preservatives; we shall learn to *know* our privileges, and duly to *value* them. There are many still among us, doubtless, who are not aware that the Reformed on the continent are not constituted, as our Church, with a liturgy, articles, homilies, and a hierarchy. While *we* are able, through God's favour, and with these helps, to enlarge our borders and extend our framework, we see those Churches, through the absence of official discipline, adding anarchy in government to anarchy in doctrine. We see daily the smaller congregations in France separating themselves from the legal consistories, of which a late number of the 'Archives du Christianisme' has presented us with a new instance. These dislocations in the Protestant body do necessarily throw out of all track the successive administrations which take the direction of affairs in that country, and all this, we fear, to the apparent benefit of Romanism, which, resting upon its three primitive creeds (the Apostles', Nicene, and Athanasian), marshals its members, and makes a bold show of success, taking no account of the unbelievers which its *fourth* creed (that of Pope Pius IV.) is engendering. Nor can the French *Englise Reformée* be much helped in its embarrassment, either by the English and American Independent Dissenters there, who animate the *Société Evangélique*, nor by the Swiss Separatists, the latter of whom, after exhibiting as sad a spectacle of confusion as it is possible for a body calling itself Christian to experience, has, it seems, at length thrown itself into the arms of Mr. Darby and the Plymouth Brethren.

" While such is the condition of those communions who have put themselves out of the pale of the Catholic Church, we see what was wanting for them to have remained in it, namely, the Episcopal institution, with the Apostolic descendancy. How far that feeling which so often broke out into the expression, ' I, Martin Luther,' impaired the fearless Reformer's work, by preventing him or his successors from keeping their eye fixed simply and steadily upon the interests of the Universal Church, can be known only to the Great Searcher of hearts. Certainly, we do not find an abiding, anxious concern for the maintenance of the visible succession. Humanly speaking, as a writer sufficiently versed in ecclesiastical polity has said—'The great mistake of the Reformation on the continent was, that Episcopacy was not preserved.' Whether it must be termed a mistake, a fault, or a misfortune, the sad consequences pervade everything, and are being constantly felt there. Nevertheless, some consolation may be formed in the thought, that although communities, like individuals, may err, still there remains the means of profiting by those lapses, and, however tardily, to retrieve what has been lost, through the experience which has been acquired. It is very evident the Reformed were all secretly inclined to Episcopacy, nor were they urged on by the spirit of *party* which is now so much put forward."—*Ibid*., pp. 145, 146.

"Under all the circumstances of the state of Europe, we might, indeed, see in Protestant— we would rather say, *true* Catholic Episcopacy (in contradistinction with *Roman* Catholic), *a bond of union,* the strongest and the most durable, between the different nations, since it would be founded upon the moral elevation and spiritual instruction of the populations, and would be a means of retrieving the abasement attendant upon superstition, as well as curbing the bad passions which spring from unbelief. The Almighty's purposes far surpass man's ken: to us only it pertains to await in entire trust and confidence, hastening their accomplishment by our prayers, and doing whatsoever His providence may set before us."—*Ibid.*, p, 154.

3. The quotations from the last article—which, in many respects, will anticipate our next subject, "The Protestant Church in France"—have been so extended, that the introductory paragraphs of the reviewer will suffice for our purpose:—

" It is with great anxiety that we look abroad throughout Europe at the present time, when Romanism is making such desperate efforts to spread and make sure her footing; when error, and infidelity, and pride, and selfishness, and luxury, and rebellion, and every evil impulse, are arising with unusual energy, and seem to be directed by the spirit of evil to destroy the simplicity and sincerity of faith, it may not be wholly unimportant to see what auxiliaries can be found in other countries for upholding those principles of true religion which it appears to be especially England's privilege to be called upon to maintain.

"France, from the important station which she occupies in the midst of Europe, seems naturally to claim our attention next after this country. In pondering upon God's ways, we would be led to desire for her, that if Great Britain be called to be the depositary and keeper, as it were, of God's truth, France might one day appear as the working power for putting that truth into action among the nations of Europe. Whoever, with an observant eye, has traversed the continent, must have remarked a gradual but general fusion of habits and manners—a universal progress in the great work of assimilation, which *must* go on increasing with the facilities for international intercourse. Taking, then, our point of departure from this our own highly favoured land—a land stationed on the limits of Europe, with a mission during the past centuries—first, to influence society politically, by that spirit of trade which, though slumbering in the rest of Europe, was preserved here for her prosperity; and now, we trust spiritually, by the purity of her Apostolic Church—taking, therefore, this point of departure, we look across the channel to see what religious elements we can find in the PROTESTANTISM OF FRANCE.

" The written controversy which has been carrying on for some time between the promoters of Separatism and the Established *Eglise Reformée* has induced us to take up a series of pamphlets, whose titles are placed at the head of this article, as being well calculated to give some idea of the state of religion in France—a subject on which it is extremely difficult for persons in this country to obtain either accurate or sufficient information. Those who are acquainted only with the Protestantism of England—where our privileged Church, at the same time she protested against the errors and abuses which overspread Europe, remained, nevertheless, *Catholic*, shaking off only the yoke of Rome with her abominations—can have very little idea of what the present Protestantism of France really is.

We purpose, therefore, first, to give a brief sketch of the mode of ecclesiastical government in the *Eglise Reformée*, and afterwards to show the circumstances which led to its present distracted state.

"Painful indeed is the view which these pamphlets present. We seek for a *Church*, and we find only unconnected heterogeneous fragments. We seek for some power of godliness capable of making head against the errors of the Romish communion, and we find, on one side, the exclusive doctrines of ultra-Calvinism—on the other, the laxity of modern Neologism, even to the rejecting the doctrine of the atonement. We seek for, at least, an outward unity, but, alas! we meet with a political separation, similar, in spirit and operation, to modern Dissent in England, using all its efforts to batter down what establishment does exist, in order to substitute in its place pure Independency, with the voluntary principle. In short, these pamphlets disclose to us the melancholy picture of a Protestant body tending to the same spirit and position as when France was ravaged by a religious civil war; when the Reformed faith being engaged in a struggle for its very existence in that country, all the aid which neighbouring powers friendly to its cause could give the Reformed might, indeed, add to their importance, as a *political body*, but never could impart the preponderancy of a *Church.*"—*Ibid*, No. xvi., October, 1840, pp. 404-406.

4. The best view of public opinion in England, which shows the increased approximation of the minds of our countrymen to their mother-Church, is amply laid open in the progressive reprints of the " Tracts of the Anglican Fathers."

" Among many of those signs of the times which encourage us to hope, and which leave on our minds a calm and quiet confidence, that God has not yet forsaken us, we look with especial thankfulness on the increasing desire to investigate deeply the principles on which the doctrine and discipline of our Church are founded. We see, it is true, that on every side the sacred citadel is assailed, and that the defenders within, like the factions of John and Simon, at the siege of Jerusalem, are but half united. We find great diversities existing among the clergy as well as the laity, and a spirit of unholy rivalry subsisting between the various parties; yet, while the bitterness remains, the number of the combatants is decreasing. One by one the sounder minded are drawing together—the " Record" on the one hand, and the " Tracts for the Times" on the other, are losing their adherents; and though the young partizans of the former are as sanctimonious and as pharisaic, and those of the latter as conceited and as insolent as ever, they excite now disgust, instead of alarm—pity, instead of indignation.

" We cannot expect that a raw youth, who has just taken his degree as Bachelor of Arts, and who has been necessitated to confine his attention to the classics, and history, and mathematics, necessary to stick, as a tail to his name, that ornamented appendage—can have, in ordinary cases, more than a mere smattering of divinity; nor can we reasonably hope that he shall see his deficiencies, if he can, by attaching himself to a party, be raised, at least in his own imagination, to some trifling degree of consequence. This intermixture of evil with good is one of the conditions of our finite nature, and' we cannot suppress it, for it is part of the evil which is in the world through sin. Notwithstanding all this, we do nevertheless rejoice that the present condition of our Church is one rather of controversy than rest. There is an Indian fable which tells us, that the water of immortality was obtained by the churning of a troubled sea; and amongst the *worthier* controversialists of our day, we have some whose exertions have done much, and will, we trust, do more, towards unveiling

'The face sublime of truth eternal.'

We have no pleasure in the larger portion of those who write expositions of our creeds and articles; not only because they have wasted, too often, their own time, and that also of their readers, but because, even if they are right, they do but say what others have said far better before them. When, however, we see reprints from our elder and mightier divines—men, the print of whose footsteps shows us how colossal was their intellectual stature—then we feel our trust encouraged and our hopes strengthened; and it may be that the study of such writings will, by God's blessing, be made the means of raising a generation of theologians to walk in their steps. The Parker Society—the Library of Anglo-Catholic Theology—the new editions of Thorndike, and Patrick, and Lawrence—Jenkyn's Cranmer—Heber's Taylor—the works of Bingham and Collier, put forth but this last year by Mr. Straker—and lastly, though not in the least place, the " Tracts of the Anglican Fathers," have worked, and are still working, a very beneficial influence on the public mind."—*Ibid.* No. xx., October, 1841, pp. 257, 258.

THE CHURCH is now manifestly the rallying point, round which the most thoughtful men cling, in the existing and almost awful state of things. Astounding discoveries in the physical world, and the strong excitement of the public mind, and other corresponding signs, render these the most interesting times since the primitive ages of Christianity, and the Reformation of the Western Church in the sixteenth century.

" No thoughtful man can now look around on what may be called the great masses of Christendom, to mark the tendency of the spirit by which they are severally actuated, without being convinced that perilous times are at hand; and that the only apparent means of averting the probable evils, or of passing safely through them, if they should arise, must be found in the Church, and this Church not only a faithful and zealous, but also an united body. Not that the masses of which we are speaking have as yet set themselves to do the evil which we foresee, or are themselves generally aware of the spirit which now impels them; but this spirit is the very opposite of that which is essential to the well-being of the Church, and as its opposite, will become its antagonist, as soon as it perceives that the Church does stand in its way. And it behoves the Church now, while there is yet time, to prepare itself for a conflict of no ordinary kind, and which can be met successfully by no ordinary preparation.

"In modern times men are brought together in larger masses than formerly, from their having, through the diffusion of knowledge, greater community of thought; and, for the same reason, they are more capable of being acted on by others, for good or for evil. But, unfortunately, they have been, for the most part, left to act upon each other, and so foster each other's evil tendencies; or have been under the influence of those whose ends were selfish, and who, for their own purposes, have made that influence a means of increasing the evil propensities of our nature, instead of counteracting them or turning them to good. These masses, left to themselves, or played on by demagogues, think only of themselves, of their own importance, and brood over it until they think themselves omnipotent; they talk of nothing less than the sovereign majesty of the people, and become in the end gods themselves. And the spirit which actuates the lower orders, and appears in this gross and palpable form amongst them, does really mount higher— does really pervade the scientific and intellectual classes, and will in all produce the same effects, though in a manner less gross and revolting, in proportion to the refinement of the classes amongst whom it is manifested.

"Who can doubt whether Chartism and Mechanics' Institutes have their counterparts among the higher classes? Or that these last are at all more diffident of their own importance, or less under the despotic sway of public opinion, than the former? We fear that there exist precisely the same evils among them, and that they are only the deeper from being the less apparent. It cannot but be so, since it has been the set endeavour and boast of modern times to divorce education from religion; and as the greater diffusion of mere secular knowledge has led to these results in the lower orders, so, the better the education, the greater will be the risk of similar results. And we fear it the more, inasmuch as, among all ranks, education and pastoral authority are dropping, by little and little, entirely out of the hands of the clergy—the watchmen and shepherds set of God for the very ends of warning against evil and guiding men in the truth.

"And the clergy should remember that the masses of which we are speaking are in the Church. God has put His name upon them in baptism, and they have taken vows to be His people; and upon the clergy God has laid the responsibility of caring for the souls of the people. Let the clergy bear continually in mind the extent of this responsibility, and, in proportion as difficulties and dangers environ the Church, so gird up their strength to meet them, and to meet them in the quarters from whence the danger arises—not to think it enough to be generally armed and prepared, as it is their duty to be at all times; but with special preparation against special dangers, expecting a special blessing from God on their endeavours—not in blind recklessness, but in the enlightened confidence of faith.

"God designed that the relationship between the clergy and people should be ever the same, and in this relationship, more emphatically than in any other, *knowledge is power;* "for the priest's lips should keep knowledge, and they should seek the law at his mouth." If the people advance in knowledge, so must the clergy—in knowledge of every kind in which the people advance; for a man cannot continue to lead unless he will keep himself the foremost. As no one can deny the fact that this age is more advanced in knowledge than any preceding age, so ought the Church to be more enlightened now than at any preceding period, and especially in the things of God; and all this knowledge may become consecrated to the service of God, and tend to the real blessing of man.

"Theology embraces everything, because everything receiving its being and the laws thereof from God, everything tells some tale concerning Him; and to show that it tells it truly is the province of theology. But theology must begin with the knowledge of Him; it is otherwise worse than an empty sound—it would be a falsehood. And the knowledge of God is only to be attained by means of the Church, to whom the mystery hid from ages and generations was first revealed, in order that through her it may be declared to all mankind. We mean not the mere knowledge that there is a God—a fact which each one of His works attests; but the knowledge of a personal God, of the Father, the Son, and the Holy Ghost, and of our true relationship to Him. This was veiled in mystery, or only shadowed forth in types, which were unintelligible till the Antitype came—till Jesus Christ revealed the Father—till He, as Head of the Church, committed the sacred deposit to those whom He had chosen, and gave them the Holy Ghost, rightly to apprehend and steadfastly to maintain that truth unto the end of the world. And by the Church we mean, not merely the living men of this or that place, or of this or that generation, but the Universal Church of all ages.

"The Church is called to the high office of standing in the councils of God, and being His interpreter to men, at all times, and according to the sense men have of their need. Paul said to the men of Athens, 'Whom ye ignorantly worship, Him declare I unto you—God that made the heavens.' He suited the instructions he gave to the state of knowledge amongst his audience; and, above all, he would not let them rest in the superstition of acquiescing under that love of mystery to which man is prone, nor let them crouch before a vague and undefined power, the creature of their imagination, but point their reverence to Almighty God. And now, when 'men run to and fro, and knowledge is increased' to an unprecedented degree, the Church must be able to speak equally to the point—the Church must take care that the people grow not too superstitious, and, instead of the unknown, declare to them the true God. And when some are making an idol of popular opinion; others are looking no further than matter and its laws; others are saying that creeds are unimportant, and conduct everything; and a more numerous party than all, which calls itself pre-eminently the Church, is resting on forms and ceremonies alone; that which is *the Church indeed* should raise its voice, and proclaim, these at the best are but secondary things—there is One above and beyond these—these are not God—worship Him."—*Ibid.*, pp. 387-390.

IV.

ANCIENT LITERATURE, AND THE FIRST NATIVE BISHOP OF ICELAND.

See Note H, Sermon, P. 58, and Appendix, P. 169.

"In general, the Danish *literati* have particularly turned their researches to the history and antiquities of the North—on which subjects many curious works have been printed, and more are preparing for public inspection. Among those who have greatly distinguished themselves in this branch of learning must be mentioned the names of Meursins, Holberg, Olaus Wormius, Pontopidan; and lately those of Langebek, Schoening, and Subm.

"Among the performances lately printed on these topics, those in the Icelandic tongue deserve particular notice, as they tend to throw considerable light on the antiquities, history, and mythology of the northern nations; Iceland being in the remote ages—while Sweden, Denmark, and Norway, were in a state of perpetual warfare—the repository of northern literature. On observing such a number of Icelandic manuscripts as are contained in the Danish libraries, I was greatly astonished to find that Iceland, considered by the ancients as the *Ultima Thule*, or the extremity of the world, and by us as scarcely habitable, abounded in learning and science, at a time when great part of Europe was involved in darkness.

" History does not ascertain the first population of Iceland; when occupied by a colony of Norwegians, in the latter end of the ninth century, it contained but few inhabitants, whose ancestors were supposed to have emigrated from England or Ireland, but whose number was inadequate to resist the invaders. Afterwards, other emigrants landing from Norway, Sweden, and Denmark, the original inhabitants were lost amid the swarm of new settlers, who introduced the ' worship of Thor and Odin, and all the rites and customs which prevailed among the nations of the neighbouring continent.' Their language was the old Gothic or Teutonic, the vernacular tongue of the Swedes, Danes, and Norwegians, which, on account of their insular situation, was preserved pure for a considerable time. The alphabet was composed of the Runic characters, only sixteen in number; yet to these Icelanders we are indebted for almost all the historical monuments of the northern nations now remaining. From them sprung the Scalds, those ancient bards who have transmitted, in their historical poems, the principal events which happened in these remote quarters of the world from the arrival of Odin to the introduction of Christianity—a period of barbarism and ignorance which, without their labours, had been totally unknown to posterity. Although these Scaldic odes blend occasionally improbable narratives with historical events, yet, as intelligent critics may separate history from fable, and truth from fiction, and being the only sources of information relative to the early affairs of the North, they must be considered as valuable monuments of antiquity. The recital also of these compositions, at public entertainments, before the princes, whose deeds they celebrated, and who, as well as many other persons present, were well acquainted with the subject of the poem, affords a collateral proof of their authenticity. Some of these odes were written in Runic characters; the far greater part, however, were only consigned to memory; but on the introduction of Christianity into Iceland, in the latter end of the ninth century, the Runic letters were exchanged for the Roman alphabet; schools were founded;

the love of science, which had in some degree maintained itself, even when the inhabitants were in a state of Paganism, revived with fresh vigour; ancient poems were collected, many chronicles digested into a regular form, and the traditions of Pagan theology rescued from oblivion. The Icelanders possessed several historians long before a single annalist appeared among the nations from whom they were descended. Their authors, Islief Are, and Sæmund, who flourished in the eleventh century, preceded Saxo-Grammaticus, and Sueno, the earliest of the Danish, Swedish, or Norwegian writers.

" It would be an interesting speculation in the theory of mankind to ascertain how it came to pass, that a people, disjoined from the rest of the world, few in number, depressed by poverty, and situated in so unfavourable a climate, should be capable, in those dark ages, of manifesting such a taste for literature. Were we better informed of certain particulars relating to the state of the North during those remote ages, we might possibly find the cause of this phenomenon, either in the poverty of the inhabitants of Iceland, which drove them to seek their fortunes in the neighbouring countries; or in the success of their first bards at foreign courts, which excited their emulation, and at the same time prepossessed strangers in their favour; or, lastly, in the nature of their republican government, in which the talent of oratory, and the reputation of superior sense and capacity, are the direct roads to dignity, respect, and preferment. To these causes may perhaps be joined the political tranquillity of Iceland: amid the civil commotions that convulsed the neighbouring nations, the inhabitants had sufficient leisure for literary occupations; and some may be induced to add the nature of their climate, which obliged them to seek for some relief against the tediousness of long nights and continued darkness.

" But to return to the Icelandic authors. The most ancient historian was Islief, Bishop of Skalholt; he was son of Gissur Albus, a person of great distinction in Iceland, and descended from the ancient kings of Denmark, who considerably promoted the establishment of Christianity. Islief was born in 1006; and having received the first rudiments of learning from his father, was sent, in the sixteenth year of his age, into Saxony, for the purpose of completing his education, and made rapid advances in several branches of knowledge. Being ordained priest, he returned to Iceland; fixed his residence at Skalholt, where his father had erected a church, and preached the Gospel with fervent and persuasive eloquence. Islief was the first native Bishop of Iceland; he was raised to that dignity in the fiftieth year of his age, at the request of the inhabitants, by particular desire of the Emperor Henry III., and during the pontificate of Leo. IX. He was consecrated by the Archbishop of Bremen, on the 6th of January, 1056; and returning the same year to Iceland, fixed the see at Skalholt, where he continued until his death, which happened in 1080, in seventy-fifth year of his age. Islief is described as a person of a dignified aspect, affable, just and upright in all his actions, liberal, and beneficent, though, from the scantiness of his income, frequently exposed to extreme penury. The fame of his learning and piety being widely diffused, many foreign bishops visited Iceland, for the purpose of receiving his instructions; and his memory was so highly revered among his countrymen, that his name was esteemed synonymous to sanctity and erudition. He married Dalla, daughter of Thorwaldus, by whom he had three sons, all celebrated for their talents and knowledge; but particularly Gissur, who succeeded his father in the bishopric, and inherited his zeal for the propagation of the Gospel and the promotion of learning. Islief guarded against the decline of literature in Iceland, by assiduously instructing many pupils, some of whom became eminently distinguished, and two were advanced to the Episcopal dignity. He was well versed in the history of the North, and compiled several annals, which, though now lost, furnished materials for the chronicles of the earliest Icelandic authors, whose works are extant. I allude to Are, surnamed the Sage, who was educated by Tetius, son of Islief; Sæmunal Sigfurson, for his great erudition denominated Polyhistor; and Snorro Sturleson, styled by his learned editor, the Herodotus of the North; all of whom immediately succeeded Islief, and wrote on the history of Norway."—*Coxe's Travels in Poland, Russia, Sweden, and Denmark*, vol. v., pp. 148-155. Octavo. London, 1802.

www.ingramcontent.com/pod-product-compliance
Lightning Source LLC
Chambersburg PA
CBHW080051190426
43201CB00035B/2158